Catch the Sea

By Mary Haynes

BRADBURY PRESS
NEW YORK

For Francine, the merwoman,
and Irwin, the sailor

The excerpt from "Look Before You Leap" by W. H. Auden is reprinted
from The Collected Poetry of W. H. Auden *by W. H. Auden.*
(Random House, 1945), copyright © 1945 by W. H. Auden.
Reprinted by permission of the publisher.

The excerpt from "Over the Rainbow" is reprinted from the song by
E. Y. Harburg, with music by Harold Arlen, copyright © 1938,
1939 (Renewed 1966, 1967) by Metro-Goldwyn-Mayer, Inc.
Reprinted by permission of CPP/Belwin, Inc.

Bradbury Press
An Affiliate of Macmillan, Inc.
866 Third Avenue, New York, NY 10022
Collier Macmillan Canada, Inc.

Printed and bound in the United States of America
First Edition
10   9   8   7   6   5   4   3   2   1
The text of this book is set in Garamond No. 3.
Book design by Julie Quan

LIBRARY OF CONGRESS CATALOGING-IN-PUBLICATION DATA
Haynes, Mary.
Catch the sea.
Summary: *While her artist father is away trying to arrange a much-*
needed exhibition, thirteen-year-old Lily stays alone at the beach cottage
in which they've spent the summer and discovers her own inner strengths
and resources and some evidence of an artistic talent that she's always
been afraid to test.
{1. Artists—Fiction.   2. Beaches—Fiction.
3. Fathers and daughters—Fiction.   4. Self-perception—
Fiction.   5. Family problems—Fiction.}   I. Title.
PZ7.H3149148Cat   1989   {Fic}   88-26203
ISBN 0-02-743451-6

CONTENTS

1 · *Thursday after Labor Day*

The sea, the sky, the sand—they gleamed and glittered. Another perfect day. Only it was the Thursday after Labor Day, and Lily Maxwell should have been in school . . . somewhere.

Instead, she was sitting by the water on a green-and-white plastic chair, staring at the ocean, hypnotized by the waves. She and her father had been at this beach for three months. They were supposed to be moving soon, but right now they were stuck. And somewhere, eighth grade was starting without her.

Lily glanced back at the cottage where her father was happily working on another painting. She thought, I'm going to have to do something . . . and didn't move.

A high breaker crashed and came rushing toward her, and Lily put up her feet to let the wave swirl under her chair. She'd rather take action than wait, but there wasn't anything she could do, really. Lily had known for a long time: Being the daughter of artists wasn't always easy.

Her father, O. J. Maxwell, had been a painter since before Lily was born. He was beginning—or so it seemed, maybe—to be successful. To Lily's surprise his work had actually begun to sell. In addition, there had been a one-year fellowship to an artists' colony and an article about him in an art journal. And now this beach—with the Maxwells' expenses paid by a rich patron.

As far as Lily could see, success for O.J. was about the same as failure. The Maxwells squeaked by financially, and O.J. kept on painting.

Lily liked the fact that her father was an artist. She admired his work, enjoyed the ups and downs of his enthusiasms and the peculiar way he saw things.

Her mother wasn't so easy to think about. Flora Maxwell was an artist, too. But she was gone. She'd been the star student in art school before she married O.J. and had Lily . . . and decided family life wasn't for her. When Lily was four months old, Flora had packed up and moved to Paris, where she eventually became well known as a jewelry designer.

Because of this, Lily knew her mother mostly by reputation. The woman sent occasional letters, came to America for whirlwind visits. Once, when she was ten, Lily had gone to Paris for the summer. Flora had been bossy, opinionated, beautiful. She'd peered at Lily with puzzled frowns and remarked to friends, "The child might have come from a different planet. Isn't she amusing?" Very busy with work, Flora had forgotten about Lily for long periods of time, then returned to their hotel with lavish gifts, smiles, explanations. Lily had never been so miserable.

The tide was sinking her chair legs now, but Lily didn't notice. She swished the water with her hand. Sometimes she secretly wondered, What about me? O.J. and Flora are both so good. Could I ever be an artist, too? Would I want to? As always, she put the thought aside. It wasn't a question she could answer.

A huge wave broke, rippled up the side of Lily's leg, and splashed into her lap, leaving a thin residue of sand. "Yecch," she exclaimed, brushing at her thighs. She pulled the chair out of the water's way, telling herself, Come on, kid, get moving. Then she stood for a moment, shielding her eyes. Except for a fisherman and a few sunbathers far up the way, the beach was deserted, the vacationers gone.

How can Dad keep on painting? Lily wondered. She bounced in place, disturbing the sand, wishing she could figure out a way to take action.

The problem was Mrs. Pearl Phipps, O.J.'s patron. She'd been around for most of the summer, dropping in, checking up. Asking questions, even though she knew O.J. wouldn't show his work until he was done. That was their agreement; it was always his rule.

Then, three weeks ago, she'd announced, "Well,

my dears, I need a vacation. I'm off on safari. Be back around Labor Day."

"Well?" Lily asked the wind. "It's past Labor Day. Where is she?"

A row of cottages dotted the ocean front as far as Lily could see. Only two were occupied: the Maxwells' and the one next door to the north, owned by Guy Franklin, a man her father's age who'd become their friend. He stayed at the beach all year writing books.

Go talk to Dad, Lily told herself.

She set off, then paused, suddenly detecting activity at a cottage three doors down to the south. A woman was taking shutters from windows that had been boarded up all summer long. After opening the last of them, she crossed to the edge of her deck, leaned on the rail, and gazed at the sea.

Wonder if she's got kids, Lily thought. Boy, that'd help. Somebody to hang out with.

There wasn't a sign of others. The woman saw Lily and waved, then resumed her study of the ocean.

She seems happy to be here, Lily thought as she dragged the beach chair to her own stairway. She took the steps two at a time, then trotted along the narrow wooden walkway to the outdoor shower. Rinsing her feet with water from the lower spigot, she splashed at the sand on her thighs. She was too warm and dry on top for a shower.

Her father was in the front bedroom that he'd turned into a studio, still staring at the canvas he'd

4

been staring at when she left. It didn't look any different.

The painting seemed perfect to Lily, all sea and sky, out where the ocean was dangerous. "Finished?" she asked.

"Not yet." O.J. rubbed his head but didn't move his brush. "Pretty soon."

"Okay." Lily sat on a straight-backed chair in the corner and twined a foot between the rungs. She could tell he was concentrating hard and knew she shouldn't disturb him. But she said, "Dad?"

He lowered his brush and looked at her. "Hmm?"

"Um, Mrs. Phipps. What about Mrs. Phipps?"

He jumped, startled. "Is she here?"

"No, no. I was just worried."

"Oh." He grinned at Lily. "You scared me." He glanced back at the canvas, torn between Lily and whatever it was he'd been thinking. "You need something? You all right?"

Lily hesitated. Now that she was here, her questions didn't seem so urgent. "I'm fine." She settled herself more comfortably. She was the only person O.J. ever allowed to watch him work. "Paint."

Her father nodded and returned to the canvas. He squeezed yellow from a tube, mixed it with some other oils that were already on the palette, wiggled the color onto his brush, then paused.

Lily watched, but he didn't move. Her attention wandered.

Mrs. Phipps, she thought. What if she got lost on her safari? What if she fell off her elephant, died or something? What would we do then?

She thought back to last spring, when they'd first met the woman.

Until a little over a year ago, O.J. and Lily had lived in San Francisco. He had worked part time and painted. She had gone to school, played baseball in the park, enjoyed the city. Then O.J. was accepted into the Fellows Colony, a place for artists to live and work in New England. "It was fantastic," he told anyone who asked. ("Just okay," Lily amended. "I'd give it a C . . . C+ tops.")

In May, when O.J.'s fellowship was nearly over and he was thinking about what to do next, a stranger had appeared. She was a businesswoman, a cousin related by marriage to someone connected to the colony. The woman, Mrs. Phipps, had known what she wanted: someone to paint the sea. "Handsome, interesting, valuable paintings to hang in the exclusive condominiums I'm building off the Carolina coast," she'd said.

O.J. had been recommended (he was one of the only artists at the colony who made paintings that might be called landscapes), and to Lily's astonishment, the lady had picked him. O.J. had asked Lily, "What do you think? She'll pay our way, pay a lot for the paintings when they're done." He had blinked in wonder. "I'll have a patron."

Lily had liked the idea of the beach. She had agreed, and Mrs. Phipps whisked the Maxwells off to this long, narrow, North Carolina barrier island. She installed them in a cottage, gave them money, a charge account at the local grocery, and another at an artists' supply store in Wilmington, a city thirty miles away.

It had seemed like a good idea, then. Lily had loved the beach, enjoyed the people who came and went — kids, teenagers — they'd been fun.

Now she was ready for something else. Lily missed the friends she'd had in San Francisco, the new friends she'd made last year — children of artists at the colony, kids at school. She wanted to know where she and her father were going to be living, so she could make plans, think about things.

The uncertainty made her nervous.

It's enough already, she silently told her father's back.

O.J. moved forward, dipped his brush in the smear of yellow, and made one, two soft lines on the water.

He smiled. "Hmm."

"Done?" she asked hopefully.

"I . . . dunno. Maybe." He stepped back, dropping his brush into a jar of turpentine. "What time is it? Lunchtime? You hungry?"

"Sure."

As if he couldn't quite leave the studio yet, O.J.

carried the painting—carefully because it was still wet—to a chair near the table so he could look at it while they ate.

Lily cut a tomato; her father mixed tuna, onions, and mayonnaise. They got pickles and lettuce, each knowing exactly what the other wanted. Then the two of them sat at the table that separated the kitchen from the living room. Mouth full, O.J. asked, "Well, green eyes. What's this about Mrs. Phipps?"

Lily knew that when her father called her "green eyes" he was back to the present. "When's she coming? What are we going to do next? It's after Labor Day. Everybody's at school."

"Labor Day." O.J. frowned at the painting propped on the chair opposite them. "Mrs. Phipps should be here."

"Days ago. Dad?" She had his attention now. "I have to go to school. I can't just hang around, you know. I'm not old enough."

"Time slipping away, is it?" O.J. winked. He could be very charming sometimes, but right now Lily wanted answers. She held him with her eyes. "Okay. I have been thinking. We've got two alternatives. First, I did sign some papers. I'm under contract to her. I owe her paintings; she owes me money. And of course"—this was always true—"we're almost broke. We have to wait."

"But—"

"She may want me to continue. 'Paint Charleston,'

she said. She has a house there, too. Or maybe she'll just buy these. She's paying a thousand dollars per picture, remember? Why, there are eight sea-glimpsed-through-railings paintings. And four"—he bobbed his head at the new canvas on the chair— "maybe five of the horizon. Do you realize, that's twelve or thirteen thousand dollars."

Lily couldn't help nodding along with him.

"We can't count the first one; it's trash. But even so, that's a lot of money. We could live on it a long time. Go to New York. Denny said he'd help us find a place." Denny was the artist-friend the Maxwells always stayed with. "I'd make art for the Fellows Gallery, work part time. You could go to school in Manhattan, be a regular New Yorker." He shrugged encouragingly. "You'll just . . . be a little late. We can't help it."

"Hmm," she said.

"We'll know soon. After she comes—okay?"

Lily pulled the crust from her sandwich, her thoughts a jumble. New York. Don't know if I'm ready for that. Well, what did you expect? The colony? San Francisco? Dad's finished with those places, done. That's what happens when you're an artist. You have to keep . . . finding something new.

I only wish . . . things could be that easy for me.

"Lily? You okay?"

"Sure, Dad. You know me. I get antsy."

"I know. I do, too." This time his smile swayed

her. She grinned back, and they made more sandwiches.

A few minutes later a knock came, and their neighbor, Guy Franklin, called, "Hi. Anybody home?"

"Come in, come in," O.J. answered.

"Hi," said Lily, wiping her mouth. She liked Guy. They went for long walks together when he was stuck on his writing.

"Here's your mail. I picked it up." He dropped some letters on the table. Lily shuffled through them. One was a special-looking express envelope, but there was nothing for her.

"Sit down." O.J. pointed at the remains of their lunch. "I'll mix some more tuna. You hungry?"

Guy glanced at the bowl and Lily knew what he'd say. "No, thank you, I've had lunch," he explained, right on cue. Guy never ate tuna or peanut butter or any of the things the Maxwells lived on. He was a little fancier. But he never made a fuss about it.

He looked at the painting, then away, then back out of the corner of his eye. "Uh, that a new one?"

Because O.J.'s pictures were usually out of sight, Lily didn't suppose that Guy had seen more than one or two all summer. They weren't a secret, exactly; it was just O.J.'s habit. When he was working on a painting, he didn't like to talk about it. When he was finished, he put the painting away and began thinking about the next one. Besides, he always said, he didn't care for instant critiques from friends or strangers.

Only rarely did he show his work, and then only to friends he especially respected.

Now O.J. leaned back, contemplating the canvas with a proud squint. "Yes." He barely hesitated. "It's done."

"Oh, good!" Lily exclaimed. It was always a relief when one was pronounced finished.

"Yes, I believe so." O.J. turned to Guy. "What do you think?"

"I . . ." Their neighbor studied the canvas, taking his time. It was the fifth in a series of what O.J. called "real" sea paintings. "Actually, I like it. It's brilliant. So . . . strong and eerie . . ." The bottom half of the canvas was deep ocean, out very far. A thin pink line marked the horizon, then the sky seemed to fill everything, rolling back with bright swirls of color.

"The sky really does seem to do that," Guy went on. "Meet the horizon and come racing back. Ahhhmm," his voice changed. "Did Mrs. Phipps give you any . . . instructions?"

"Yes, indeed." O.J. gulped some milk. "She wanted handsome, valuable, interesting paintings. I told her that I knew I could find interesting things here. We understood each other."

"Why do you ask, Guy?" Lily said.

"Oh, nothing . . ." He looked uncomfortable.

Lily wondered what Guy thought of the others. Before the "real" sea paintings, O.J. had done a group of what he called "sea-glimpsed-through-railings"—

the wooden angles made by deck or walkway boards, with snatches of wild sea or weather beyond. He'd been very pleased with them. Before those, he had stared at the sea, sketching. And before *that*, he did one slick painting to work out colors. It could have been a magazine ad—sand, surf, waves, sky—bang, bang, bang, like a layer cake. "Dumb-and-ugly," he called it.

Silent, Guy was toying with a spoon. Feeling unsettled, Lily worried suddenly, What about Mrs. Phipps? What if she—it was impossible—doesn't like them?

O.J. wasn't thinking along quite the same lines. "She's a great woman. My patron." He picked up the mail and noticed the express letter. "Oh, here's something from Andre at the Fellows Gallery. Let's see." He gasped with surprise. "Hey, listen. He thinks two more of my countryside paintings will sell." O.J. had been interested in chimneys at the colony—bricks against bare trees and sky. "And he loved the Polaroids I sent of the new work. Listen to this."

O.J. read aloud, "'I have a cancellation in the show that's opening on Friday. As you know, I'd planned to hang some of your work on the far wall as background. But if you can get here by Sunday with the new sea paintings, I'll feature you. You're getting hot. They'd sell. Any chance? Call me.'"

O.J. waved the letter. Then his delight faded. He regarded the new painting and shook his head. "Well, I can't. We have to wait, and these pictures belong to

Mrs. Phipps. That's our agreement. Come on, folks." He tenderly carried the canvas to the studio. "Let's go swimming."

Lily trailed the men out of the cottage thinking: Did Guy seem worried about Mrs. Phipps? He did. What else did he say? Brilliant. Is Dad really brilliant? Like Flora?

Lily stopped.

Ignoring the hot sand that burned her feet, she thought, Maybe he is. If he were a big success, would he be like her?

Never.

So what are we going to do? Stay a few more days, see what happens. I can go along with that.

A breeze touched her skin, the ocean sparkled, and out in the water Lily's father beckoned. Nearby, a ghost crab inched its way across the sand. Lily moved and it scurried back to safety. "Quick as that." She peered down its hole. "Gone."

2 · *Friday—What Else Have You Got?*

≈≈≈≈≈≈≈≈≈≈≈≈≈≈≈≈≈≈≈≈≈≈≈≈≈

Early the next morning, Lily went out to the deck, put a foot on the rail, and bent deeply, loosening her muscles. She stretched both legs, then bounced, jogging in place. Her father was on the deck, too. He'd brought a blank canvas outside, placed it on the easel, and was standing before it, immobile.

"Going running?" he asked.

"Yep. Wanna come?" Lily liked running with her father. He made it more fun.

"I'm painting."

"Painting?" she echoed. "Ha. Standing."

He grinned. "Yeah. Well, that's part of it."

"I know. See you." Lily trotted down to the beach and turned south. She jogged first to warm up, then ran near the water where the sand was hard. By the time she reached the abandoned fishing pier, she'd gone two miles. She turned back with her heart pumping and her breath coming fast. She felt truly alive and happy.

Halfway home she slowed to a walk, cooling off. Studying the sand, she stopped now and then to see whether any of the black shiny things she spied were shark's teeth, fossils that often washed up on shore. She'd vowed not to pick up anything smaller than a quarter (she had so many small ones that they filled three paper cups), but big ones were harder to find.

A mixed colony of birds scurried ahead of her, and near her cottage, they flew up. Squinting, she saw why. Someone was on the beach, the newcomer from three doors down.

As Lily approached her, the woman smiled. She was barefoot, wearing sweatpants and a T-shirt, and holding a cup of coffee. Despite her casual clothes, she looked a little formal, stiff, as if she weren't really used to relaxing on the beach.

Lily slowed and said, "G'morning."

"Hi," the lady answered. "Wonderful day, isn't it?"

Lily blurted, "Do you have any kids—teenagers?" The woman stepped back as if jolted. "I mean, here, with you?"

"No. No, I'm alone." She gestured toward Lily's cottage, where something bright and pink was moving on the deck. "That your mother?"

"No. No, my mother's f—" The words "far away" died in Lily's throat. The bright pink thing was a person. "Oh my God. It's her. See ya." Lily ran. Mrs.

Pearl Phipps was on the deck, stylishly dressed in a voluminous pink shirt and skirt, with a red turban around her head.

Speeding up the steps, Lily saw Guy hovering behind his screen door. She gave him a little wave of greeting, pulled her bathing suit down at the bottom and up at the top, wishing she had a shirt to cover herself, then walked as composedly as she could to the faucet to wash her feet.

"Hello, Miss," Mrs. Phipps said with her quick smile. She always seemed to forget Lily's name. "Hurry, Mr. Maxwell. I'm dying to see!"

"Wait a minute!" O.J. called from inside.

Lily stayed where she was. The shower's upper spigot leaked cold drops onto her shoulder, but she couldn't move. "Hello, Mrs. Phipps." Trying to buy her father some time, she added, "Did you have a nice trip?"

"Wonderful. Marvelous. The wilderness is marvelous." She gazed at Lily, and her brown eyes gleamed under heavily painted lids. "I shot a rhino."

"A wha—? You did?"

"It was a special opportunity. One was ill and they had to thin the herd." She squeezed her hands together; her bracelets jangled. "I'd give anything to shoot another. But now I'm back. Tending to business." Turning to the cottage, she called, "Mr. Maxwell!"

"Yes. Ready."

Mrs. Phipps went inside. Lily grabbed a towel from the line, wrapped it around her waist for protection, then stopped at the door, unsure if she should go in or stay out. Hesitating, she noticed that O.J. had drawn a thin yellow line across the middle of the new canvas. Inside, Mrs. Phipps exclaimed, "What? *What*? What is this? *What* are these?"

"Paintings," came O.J.'s voice.

"What?"

"My paintings. These five are of the sea and sky. They're the newest ones. The others are water glimpsed through railings. I found that perspective very interesting."

"But I asked you to paint the sea!"

"I did."

"Not this way!" Lily slipped through the door and stood by the wall, flat as a shadow. Mrs. Phipps's face was red, her mouth open in an ugly grimace. "No. Where's the surf? Where's the sand? Where's the . . . the pretty?"

O.J. was red, too, and rolling to a boil. "But you—" he began.

"I hired an artist."

"Yes!" he exclaimed. "An artist. Not a photographer. You hired a . . . a vision."

"*I wanted you to paint the sea.* Mr. Maxwell, I am decorating my new condominiums, remember? They are for sale, hundreds of thousands of dollars each. They stand above the sea in solid splendor. Do you think I

17

want this frightening water? Or those weird angles? *Boards?* No. I want works of art by a real artist. Handsome pictures, Mr. Maxwell, to hang on my beautiful walls."

O.J.'s fists were clenched. He was barely holding back his anger. "These paintings could hang anywhere."

Mrs. Phipps's voice was deadly. "What else have you got? Let me see."

Lily's father brushed into the studio and pulled the first canvas he had painted for practice from the closet. It looked more than ever like a postcard — "dumb-and-ugly" seemed a good description for it. "Only this tripe. Is this what you want?"

"Ahh," she exclaimed. "Yes, this is good."

Lily gulped. Is that what she meant by "handsome"?

O.J. stuttered, "I-i-i-it's —"

"It's *one*," Lily interrupted.

"Hush, Lily." O.J. walked to the door, and holding out a hand, tried to usher Mrs. Phipps from the room. "Never mind. We'll go. I'll take my work and go. You can find another artist."

A pause.

Then Mrs. Phipps shook her head with a tight little smile. "Not so fast, Mr. Maxwell. I brought you here and paid your expenses. Didn't get a lick of rent for this cottage all summer. Just paid a huge grocery bill that you and this child ran up. Do you think I did all that for free? You'll have to reimburse me, or the paintings are mine. All of them."

"B-but what will you do with them?"

"That's my concern. I . . . I'll burn them. Or" — she gazed at the window with her arms tight across her chest— "throw them in a basement somewhere. As the wet and mold get them, I'll remember this stupid mistake."

"No! Lady, you—"

"Daddy!" Lily knew he would say things that were unforgivable. "Please!"

O.J. was trembling with rage. He grabbed a book from the sofa and flung it at the kitchen, where it hit the refrigerator with a bang. "Aaaaaargh!" he bellowed, and leaped out the door. As he ran across the deck and down to the beach, his steps shook the house.

In the silence that followed, Lily was afraid to breathe. She watched the door and listened, but O.J. didn't come back.

Mrs. Phipps watched the door, too. "Well!" she said through her teeth and looked around the room at the paintings. "All right, Miss. Help me load these."

Lily didn't think she understood. "What?"

"I won't pay him. I'll just take all these pictures and you two get out. We'll call it square."

"Oh no." Lily knew she had to stop her. "What will you do with them?"

"That's my business."

Mrs. Phipps picked up a painting. It was a recent

one, and Lily knew it was still slightly wet—oils take a long time to dry. "Careful!" she warned. "They're not dry yet."

Mrs. Phipps jumped, held the canvas more gingerly, but didn't slow down. "Come on, help," she insisted, balancing the first one by the door and going back for a second.

Stop her, Lily thought. But how? "Ah, Mrs. Phipps? Did the paintings surprise you?"

"Surprise me? I should say so." She paused. Lily was tall for thirteen, but Mrs. Phipps towered over her. "What a disaster! It's my own fault. I should have insisted on seeing what he was doing during this summer. No wonder he kept them secret."

"He doesn't let people see anything until it's finished," Lily said. "Not ever. And you agreed, remember?" Mrs. Phipps sniffed. "It's like . . . a rule."

"Not my rule! And why did he make things like these?" She flung her hands, indicating all the paintings with one wide gesture.

"Didn't you . . . see his work before?"

Mrs. Phipps didn't seem to hear the question. "Cousin Stanley told me O. J. Maxwell was good. Told me he was 'up-and-coming.' " She peered down at Lily. "Did I see his paintings? Yes, of course. He was a hundred times better than the others."

Lily couldn't help grinning. All of the artists at the colony had been very serious, but some had been a lot more unusual than O.J: making paintings in white on white, weaving fabric and strips of colored canvas into designs that Lily thought were interesting (though lumpy), or building constructions with hundreds of pieces and blinking lights.

"At least your father could paint a tree that looked like a tree. A wall that looked like a wall. I thought that when he came here, he'd paint a sea that looked like the sea." Mrs. Phipps touched dumb-and-ugly, her expression woeful, as if she really liked it.

Lily bit a finger and wondered, Would Dad make more dumb-and-uglies? Could I get him to? I don't think so. Maybe he'd do something, but not those.

Mrs. Phipps went on. "I should have known. Should have asked. You have to watch workmen every minute."

Lily said, "He could make you something."

"Even then things go wrong," Mrs. Phipps continued, not listening, as usual. "Oh, I wish I were back in Africa."

"He *is* a good painter," Lily announced staunchly.

The woman's lip curled. "That man couldn't paint his way out of a paper bag. Though . . . they say he's making a reputation. . . ."

"He's hot in New York. You'd—" be surprised. Lily didn't want to say too much. She just added, "Please?"

"Please what?"

"Don't take the paintings. Give him a little more

time." Lily wished her father would come back. Where was he? "Right now he's in shock."

"In shock? He's not the only one." Mrs. Phipps rubbed her face, smearing her makeup. "You two aren't my only problem. Things went wrong everywhere. I never should have left." For the first time she seemed almost nice. Then she pulled herself together. "Find me a piece of paper."

Lily hurried to comply. Mrs. Phipps flipped open her handbag, took out a gold pen, and scrawled a note. She handed it to Lily, who quickly read:

> You have one week.
> I want *good* paintings.
> I'm seeing my lawyers.
> PP

"Give that to your father. Tell him to do what I say or I'll get the law after him." She turned, her skirts swirled, and she was gone.

The ocean roared; a car passed. Numb and wobbly, as if she'd stepped off a roller coaster, Lily went outside. She wasn't used to dealing with people like Pearl Phipps all by herself.

Guy tiptoed out of his front door and called across the distance between the two cottages, "Lily?"

"Yeah?"

"What happened?"

"She hates them. She and Dad had a terrible fight.

She almost took the paintings, just to throw away. Did you see which way he went?"

Guy pointed north. "Up there."

Lily saw a few indistinguishable specks in the distance. "Guy . . . it was awful."

"I was afraid of that," he said. "Mrs. Phipps . . . doesn't have much imagination."

"You tried to warn him."

"He didn't hear me. I should have insisted. I . . . hoped I was wrong."

One of the specks on the beach took shape—Lily's father, waving his arms. "There he is. I better go see." She ran as fast as she could, and he stopped when she approached, his hands dangling at his sides.

"Um, hi," she said. Wide-eyed, O.J. looked horribly like he was going to cry. "Dad? It's okay. She . . . she's just a yuck-ball. She . . . shoots rhinoceroses."

"I can't believe I was so stupid. I'm a terrible—"

"No, you're not."

"Idiot."

Lily repeated, "You're not. Honest, Dad."

There was three feet between them, an unbridgeable gulf, until O.J. murmured, "Oh, Lily," and held out his arms.

She hugged him, speaking into his shirt, "Are you all right?"

"I . . ." They started walking. "I keep seeing her face. That awful grimace when she said, 'No.' "

"She, she's—"

"I don't know what to do." He turned to Lily, his mouth white at the corners. "I don't know why I think I . . . know everything."

Lily clung to his arm. "You know a lot," she told him, but he didn't seem to agree.

At the cottage he rinsed his feet and nodded a greeting to Guy. "Guy. Lily. Excuse me a moment." The screen door banged behind him.

Lily whispered, "What should I do?" Her father had been upset before, but never like this.

"Let him be," Guy advised. "For now."

"Okay." Lily went inside. O.J. was in his bedroom flinging things around and slamming dresser drawers. Then he went into the bathroom, closed the door, and turned on the shower.

Lily waited. It was a long shower, but every once in awhile he bellowed "Yeah?" or "Oh no!" so she figured he was all right. Then the water stopped. The bathroom was quiet for so long that Lily crept to the door and knocked. O.J. came out and squeezed past her, saying, "It's okay, honey. I'm going to sleep."

She started to speak. "Ah, Mrs. Phipps . . . there's a note—" But he went straight into the bedroom without stopping.

Lily heard the bed creak, then silence. She went out to the deck and saw Guy at the table where he did his writing, by the ocean window. He opened it. "What's up?" he called.

24

"He won't talk. He's going to sleep."

"I'll be right over."

They went straight into O.J.'s bedroom and stood by the bed. O.J. seemed to stiffen and his mouth got tighter. Guy cleared his throat and said, "Maxwell?"

O.J. frowned and shifted. "I never thought . . . I can't believe I could be so dense. I was so happy to have a patron, someone to buy things for sure. I should have known she wanted ones like that first one—" He waved toward the studio. "Anybody could do them. A child . . ."

Lily shook her head. She couldn't paint that well, and *she* was a child (or had been not long ago). Sometimes her father had funny ideas. When she was much younger, she'd spent many hours in the studio daubing away in a corner with her own tubes of paint. She'd never made anything remotely like O.J.'s dumb-and-ugly painting. Her father sat up, his head in his hands.

Guy said, "They are good, you know."

O.J. looked blank.

"Your paintings. Your real paintings."

Lily's father got up and washed his face, then sat at the dining room table. Lily and Guy followed. "Yes, Guy? You really think so?" He seemed so uncertain that Lily's heart went out to him.

"Indeed," said Guy. "There's vigor. A sense of the power of the sea, the strength of nature. And our frail railings . . . there are ideas in your paintings."

"I can't let her have them. I can't do that."

"No," said Guy and Lily at once.

"What we're going to have to do"—O.J. was drawing quick, slashy boxes on an old newspaper—"is leave. Pack up. Get out of here. Just . . . run."

"No, Dad. Listen." Lily explained about her conversation with Mrs. Phipps.

"She almost took the paintings?" O.J. was getting mad again.

"And she said she wouldn't pay?" asked Guy. "I don't think she can do that. You should get a lawyer."

"*She's* getting a lawyer." Lily handed over the note.

O.J. read it. "A week? *Good* ones?" He crumpled the message. "What does she think? That in a week I can make stacks of paintings? Ones I hate?"

Lily was afraid he'd say that. "Can't you . . . try?"

He shook his head. "No." Clenching his pen, O.J. drew squares and more squares on the piece of newspaper. "I want to go. For a week, no more. Get the paintings to New York. Get them in the show. Then see."

"Oh, Daddy." Lily hardly ever called him Daddy, but this time it slipped out. "We can't."

He stopped drawing. "What if we left the lights on? She wouldn't know. She'd think we were here."

"She'd know," said Guy. "She'd find out. Mrs. Phipps can be relentless, you know."

"I'm sorry I ever signed up with her!" O.J. cried.

"What can I do?" He threw down his pen, strode to the ocean window, and stared out.

Lily had never seen her father so dejected. As if he were a stranger, she studied his back. She noticed that his hair was getting long again, curls tumbling toward his collar. His shirt—faded madras—was half untucked. She felt sorry for him. His problems were so big and complicated.

My problems are different, she thought. I was so anxious to move and get settled somewhere. But now—

An idea made her shiver. We don't have to . . . both go. Without pausing for conditions or doubts, she said, "Hey, Dad, I've got it." He didn't stir. "You go to New York and sell some paintings. I'll stay here. I'll pretend you're here, too. Fool her."

He turned. "Oh no."

"Why not?"

"I couldn't leave you."

"For a week? I'd be all right." She suppressed a smile. Might be fun. The image of Pearl Phipps— angry, difficult—flashed into Lily's mind, but she ignored it.

Guy said, "Hmm! That's not a bad idea. But you couldn't stay alone, Lily. You'd have to stay with me."

Lily leveled him with a stare. "No, I need to be here. So when Mrs. Phipps comes, I can send her away."

"But—" Guy began.

Shaking his head, O.J. came back to the table. "No, honey."

Lily stuck out her chin. "Why not?"

Guy spoke slowly. "I could watch out for her. I'd be right next door."

O.J. looked from one of them to the other, rubbing his cheek. Lily was bursting. Her idea seemed perfect. She covered her mouth to keep from speaking while her father made up his mind. She knew from experience that if she said too much, she'd blow it. "You'd . . . just stay here?"

Her response was clipped and certain. "Yep."

"And Guy, you'd watch out for her?"

"Of course."

"While I . . . went to New York, got in the show, sold paintings." He'd begun to smile.

Paintings, Lily thought, realizing there were some holes in this plan. "Um, Dad? Could you make some of those ones she likes while you're gone?"

"Me? I'd be busy." He stopped before Lily, his eyes searching. "I'd call you at Guy's, leave plenty of groceries. You'd be careful? Lock the doors? You sure?"

She nodded solemnly. He hesitated and she held very still. He had to say yes.

O.J. reached up as if he could hug the world. "All right then! We'll worry about Mrs. Phipps later. I'll pack up the paintings, all but that one she likes and the last one—it's far too wet."

"Better take my car," Guy offered. His small station wagon was much more dependable than the Maxwells' 1972 VW bus. "I got gas today."

"You mean it?" O.J. shook Guy's hand with both of his. He was dancing in place. "I'll call Andre and tell him I'm coming. The opening's next Friday. I've got just a week and there'll be a thousand things to do. But maybe . . . it'll work."

"It will," Lily assured him, caught up in his excitement. The cottage seemed full and happy. Anything was possible. "Only, there should be painting happening here. Can you paint, Guy?"

He shrugged. "I flunked fifth-grade art. Can't draw at all."

Lily hadn't painted for a long time. She knew better than to call herself an artist. But she thought of the empty studio and said, "Leave instructions on how to mix the colors for dumb-and-ugly, Dad. Okay?"

3 · Day, Night, Day—Alone

In the next few hours, O.J. asked Lily a hundred times, "Are you sure?" while he made preparations in a flurry. He bought groceries (paid for with their own scant funds). There was no phone in the Maxwells' cottage, so he gave Lily a list of emergency numbers and some money. "Use the pay phone down the beach road. Or use Guy's and we'll pay him back," he said. "Now remember to lock the doors. And don't swim alone. And . . . just give Pearl Phipps the brush-off."

From Guy's cottage he telephoned Andre, who said, "Good!" and his friend Denny in New York, who said, "Great. Love to see you."

At last he was ready.

Guy helped load the last of the paintings—carefully—then shook O.J.'s hand, and said, "Good luck. I . . . was in the middle of a chapter today when all this came up. Best get back to it." He went into his cottage.

The Maxwells looked at each other. "This is it, Lily," O.J. said. "Change your mind?"

"No." She couldn't now even if she wanted to. "Call Guy's when you get there?"

"I will. I don't know how long it'll take. I'll pull over when I get sleepy."

"Be careful."

They hugged, then he climbed into the car and drove away, tooting his horn long after he was out of sight.

Lily stayed in the street until he was absolutely gone. Then she went into the cottage and wandered from room to room. There was a peculiar new silence in the air. She warmed some leftovers for dinner, flipped through the new magazine her father had surprisingly bought for her, washed the dishes and . . . discovered she wasn't used to being alone.

She went out to the deck. Guy's lights were on, and she could hear his typewriter pounding. Busy. She couldn't always glom onto him. She had to manage by herself.

Lily sat down and looked through the railing at the ocean. She wiggled her toes toward the sea and thought, What will I do?

First, she decided, she liked the idea of staying alone. She loved her father, but his work, his compulsions and confusions took up a lot of space. She wouldn't mind just . . . being for a while. Filling her own space.

Peering through the railing at some people who were passing by, out for an evening stroll, Lily thought, they're happy. Why not? Enjoy the beach. Get to know whoever comes along.

Next she thought of the studio. The new canvas with one thin yellow line painted across the middle. Lily felt a little shiver of anticipation. She made an appointment with herself: tomorrow.

The only problem was Mrs. Phipps. It had been easy to volunteer "I'll fool her," to think of brushing her off like a crumb. But would it be easy? Every time Lily thought back to their conversation that afternoon, she was amazed at how brave she'd been. She wasn't sure she could do it again.

Maybe Mrs. Phipps won't come around, Lily told herself hopefully. After all, she said a week.

Lily went back inside the cottage and flipped on the small black-and-white TV. She used its flickering images to fill the room because, even with big plans, the night was spooky.

At twelve-thirty she was too sleepy to stay up any longer. After checking the locks, Lily turned off the lights, climbed into bed, and lay like a board, wide awake.

The cottage creaked. It had never been so noisy

before. What's that? Burglars? Every time Lily started to relax, a new sound came.

Finally too exhausted to care, she crept out of bed, opened the window an inch so she could hear the ocean, put a pillow over her head, and fell asleep.

At dawn the sun, huge and orange-red, was poking up at the edge of the horizon. It's early, Lily thought. The cottage was so silent that it was as if ten people, not just one, had left. Whistling to fill the air, she turned on the teakettle, got into her swimming suit, and took a cup of tea to the deck to watch the rest of the sunrise. The world was pink and orange and blue. You'll get used to the quiet, she told herself. There was a whole day ahead.

When the sun was five or six inches above the horizon and had shrunk to yellow-white once more, Lily noticed someone bobbing in the water out beyond the breakers.

It's that lady, Lily thought.

She got a towel and headed across the sand, danced over a few shallow ripples, then paused. The woman saw her.

"Hi," Lily called. "Water nice?"

"Yes."

"Um, could I swim with you?" Lily swallowed her pride and explained across the distance, "I promised not to swim alone."

The woman took a step toward Lily. A huge wave dunked her and she came up laughing. "Come on. It's more fun with two."

Another wall of water rose. Lily dove through. Her neighbor was wearing an aqua flowered swimsuit. She had lots of freckles and her reddish hair was in her eyes.

All summer Lily had made friends with kids at the beach—it was as easy as stepping into water. But she'd never swum with a strange grown-up before and wondered, How do you act?

"Hi," she said, sticking out a hand. "I'm Lily Maxwell. I live over there."

"Anna Herbert." The woman shook Lily's hand firmly. "You say you're alone?"

"No! No, I—" Anna Herbert's gaze was level. Somehow, it seemed better not to lie. "Not ex . . . actly. Will you be here long?"

"Pretty long. One semester."

Lily thought, Funny way to tell time.

Just then the water curled high. Anna Herbert yelled, "Watch out!" and they both dove through.

Lily loved it when the waves were big. "Try to jump them when you can. It's fun. More scary."

They did that for a while, then the woman went out deeper and lay floating, her eyes closed.

Lily floated, too, for a while, but it was boring. She went back to daring the surf. Suddenly she miscalculated and was grabbed, twisted, and smacked to the bottom. Flailing underwater, she banged the sand, bobbed up, got a gasp of air, then was sucked under again. Emerging at last, she snuffled hard—half the ocean was up her nose—and rubbed her shoulder. "Thought I was a goner."

Anna Herbert had stopped floating and was watching Lily with concern. "Ever bodysurf?" the woman asked as she edged along where the waves formed, with her eyes out to sea. When a big one loomed, she caught it and sped like a torpedo toward the sand.

"Wow," said Lily, then yelled, "Neat, Mrs."—she didn't know what to call her—"ah, Mrs? . . . Herbert."

"Mrs. will be fine," said the woman, rejoining Lily. "You like to bodysurf?"

"Oh yes."

"Then let's."

They stood in place, waiting. When a good wave came, Lily yelled, "Go!" She wasn't going to be left behind this time. Swimming hard, she felt the water surge and flung out her arms, head down, kicking until she was lifted and sent, *swoosh*, far into shore.

Mrs. Herbert was right with her. They both laughed and went back to try again.

Before long Mrs. Herbert said, "That's enough swimming for me. I'll turn into a prune."

"Okay," Lily replied, hiding her disappointment.

She could have swum for another two hours, at least. As they waded in to shore, Lily glanced at her cottage. In the bright light of morning she wasn't so sure that Mrs. Phipps would stay away. "I better get back," she said. "Thank you. That was fun."

"I liked it, too," said Mrs. Herbert, rubbing her hair with a towel. "See you later."

I'm starving, Lily decided when she got home. She downed a peanut butter sandwich and a huge glass of milk, then looked at the clock on the stove. It was only nine-thirty. All of a sudden, time seemed to be moving so slowly. Lily missed her father. Well, I'm not gonna get lonesome. I have . . . stuff to do.

She went into the studio. O.J.'s barely started canvas was there, propped on the easel. Lily faced it.

Me? Make a painting? Why?

The topmost reason was Mrs. Phipps. Lily didn't expect that she could make something that would suit the woman. Not for a minute. But she had a kind of superstitious sense that she could manage things better, handle Mrs. Phipps better, if she could say, "Yes, the painting is begun."

That was one reason. The main one was different.

Lily was . . . curious. Her parents were artists. And she, so far as she knew, was not. With no one around to watch, she wanted to find out if that was really true.

It had been years since she'd messed around in her

father's studio and . . . she'd kind of liked painting then. She'd never shown much drawing talent in school (her art teachers had always been *too* interested). But she'd watched her father, known about her mother, and had her secret questions: Did any of their ability rub off? Would I like to be an artist? Now would be a good time to find out. If nothing else, she told herself, it'll pass the time.

Staring at the canvas, however, Lily wasn't optimistic. O.J. had written down how he'd mixed the colors for the dumb-and-ugly painting. She trailed her fingers along the blank surface. Sand here, water there, sky up on top.

She got out the paints, lined them up, got a clean, dry brush, and squiggled it against her cheek. Weak at the thought of beginning, she decided, I'm not ready. Take a walk.

She turned north, away from Mrs. Herbert's, and splashed happily along the water's edge. There were only a few people around. She passed a fisherman she'd seen many times before and greeted him as always, "Catching any?"

"Nawp," he said with a grunt. "Not many."

The tide was out. She walked farther than she ever had, found six fairly good shark's teeth, and dropped them one by one down the front of her swimming suit for safekeeping. A group of seven pelicans flew by. They moved so slowly that they seemed almost to hang suspended in the air. Lily shaded her eyes to squint at them. She really liked pelicans. She'd heard they were common in some places, like Florida. Here they were seen only on the wing, never walking, and always made her feel lucky.

When she turned back, she was surprised to see by the sun that it was after noon. Halfway home she met Guy Franklin. He said, "I saw you go and thought I'd try to catch up."

So much for total isolation, Lily thought, and grinned at Guy. He was wearing rolled-up white pants that were wet around the bottoms. "I found some good shark's teeth."

"That's nice. O.J. called."

"He did? When?"

Guy studied the sky. He told time by the sun the same way Lily did. (She'd learned from him.) "About an hour ago. He got to New York this morning. Everything seems like it'll work out. He'll call again soon, or you call him collect, he said. You can use my phone."

"I'm sorry I missed him."

"I know." They walked in silence for a while, then Guy asked, "Is it hard, being alone?"

"No." Lily's voice had a small, telltale wobble. "There's this new lady down the beach. Anna Herbert. I went swimming with her."

"Anna Herbert? Really?"

"Yes. Why?"

"She's usually too busy to come here. Teaches at a university."

"What?" Lily couldn't imagine swimming with a college professor. "Teaches what?"

"Astronomy, astrophysics—something like that. Isn't it time for school to be in session?"

"She said something about being here a semester."

"Hmm." Guy gazed toward the professor's cottage, now almost in view. "Dr. Herbert must be on sabbatical this fall."

"Doctor?"

"Of course. Not a physician. A Ph.D."

Lily was astonished. She was pretty sure she'd never be able to go swimming with Mrs. Herbert again. She'd feel too dumb. "How do you know her?"

"All of us owners get to know each other, eventually. Once the summer folk go."

Lily understood. She'd made a lot of one-week, two-week friends this summer. They had come and gone like the tide. Nearby only Guy had remained constant, settled in his cottage like he'd stay forever. "Do you ever go? Live somewhere else?"

"Sometimes." He smiled. "This beach is a good place to write. When I'm in the middle of a book, I keep at it."

"Do you have one I could read?"

"Maybe. I think there's some old copies around.

Give you one at dinner tonight, how's that? Want to come?"

She thought of how she didn't want to bother him . . . and of the peanut butter sandwich she'd planned to have. "I can eat at home."

"I know."

Dragging a toe to make her footprints funny, Lily thought it over. "Okay. Thanks. I'd like to."

When they got in sight of their cottages, Guy gestured toward the large, two-story house that stood on the right-hand side next to his. "Too bad the Blakes aren't here."

"Who's that?"

"My neighbor, Owen, and his three kids. He hardly ever sees them, but they come sometimes in September."

The big house was empty. Lily remembered seeing a man there before, and a woman, but never anyone else. She assured Guy, "Don't worry about me. I don't need kids. Really. I'm fine."

At home Lily's cottage seemed emptier, if that was possible. It was only two o'clock.

All right, Lily, she told herself. You said you wanted to paint? So paint.

She went to the studio, glared at the easel, and wondered what she remembered about oils. She'd never tried them before. When she was younger, her father had given her acrylics because he said they were easier to work with.

But real artists use oils, so I will.

She decided to start at the top with the sky and squeezed out an array of blues. She opened the turpentine to thin the paint. The smell was strong and familiar—like home. Gonna be a disaster, she told herself cheerfully, and started in.

After daubing some color onto the upper left corner, Lily went out to look at the sky, then realized it could be as many different ways as anyone could possibly ever imagine. Try first to get the upper section all blue, she told herself. You can paint over oil, so it shouldn't hurt. . . .

Guy made stuffed flounder and salad and tiny biscuits for dinner. Lily minded her manners and kept one hand in her lap. She felt awkward. Even though she'd known Guy all summer, she didn't think she'd ever eaten alone with him, and it seemed strange, formal somehow, more an "occasion" than just dinner.

Guy didn't seem to notice. He told funny stories about a trip he'd made to Mexico when everything went wrong and how he'd had a wonderful time anyway. When they were almost through, Lily asked, "Did you really fail art in school?"

"In fifth grade. They started drawing people that looked like people, and I was still doing stick figures.

They seemed nice to me, but the teacher said I wasn't trying. I got obstinate, and then she said I was disruptive." He chuckled. "I guess I was. I remember a lot of book dropping and spitballs."

"You remember all that?"

"I've been thinking about it since your father left. Are you really going to paint?"

"I'm trying." Smoothing her napkin, Lily remembered the canvas she'd left: a sticky blue disaster. "It'll probably end up in the trash."

"You don't sound very sure of yourself. Didn't you . . . inherit?"

"I don't know. I take art in school, but I never make anything good. Dad says he was drawing all the time when he was a kid. And M—my mother won a statewide contest in Oregon where she lived when she was ten. I've been wondering if it got passed down. The talent. Maybe it skipped a generation."

"That happens. Then you'll have other talents."

Lily twisted her fingers. "Yeah."

Guy went to the kitchen and came back with a thawed coconut cake. "Your mother. O.J. never talks about her."

As always, Lily froze. She didn't like being asked about Flora. But Guy was a good friend, easy to talk to. And Flora had been in Lily's thoughts lately.

"Dad doesn't talk about her?" Lily shrugged. "Isn't it silly? She makes us nervous. She . . . left when I was a baby. They were in art school together. They got

42

married and had me and . . . she couldn't stand it. Being confined. Being 'stuck on the West Coast.' Dad says she thought life there moved too slowly. She ran off, all the way to Paris, and was"—Lily could hear her mother's voice telling the story—"living in one tiny room, making jewelry and selling it on the street. She got discovered, got famous almost overnight."

"That's remarkable."

"Right." It wasn't remarkable to Lily. "So she was gone. They got a divorce. Dad has custody. I . . . I used to think he should get married again, so we could forget her"—the idea of Flora Maxwell loomed as always, unforgettable—"only . . . he doesn't, we don't."

"He's wary."

So am I, I guess. "We hardly ever see her and when we do—"

"Hmm?"

Lily made a face. "It's no fun. We . . . don't like her much. Sometimes she sounds sort of friendly now. But I don't believe her." Lily changed the subject. "Done? I'll help you with the dishes."

Jumping to clear the table, she kept her chin down and her face tight. The thought of Flora Maxwell always made her feel hot and unhappy when . . . she wasn't unhappy at all.

"What about you?" she asked brightly as she nodded toward the typewriter. "Get a lot of work done today?"

"Pretty much."

Thinking of his writing, Lily said, "Hey, you promised—"

"A book." He seemed pleased that she'd remembered and reached in a cardboard box behind the sofa to pull out a paperback, *Guns on the Sierra*, by Adam West.

Lily took it. She noticed the box was full of identical copies. "That's you? Adam West?"

"Yes, ma'am."

"You write—"

"Westerns."

"While looking at the ocean."

"The Atlantic. Because it's really"—he tapped his forehead—"in here. When I look out, sometimes instead of the sea, I see . . . a horseman riding across a plain, a bad guy hiding behind a rock. When they reach each other . . . they're all I know or hear."

"Neat," said Lily. He inscribed the book, "To Lily, who will find her talent. From her good friend, Adam West."

She took the book home, made sure the streetside door was locked, then went out to the deck to sit on the top step and watch the night come.

First day is over, Lily thought, hugging her knees. Listening to birds call each other home through the darkness, she leaned against the rail and thought, Daddy.

Even after all day, she hadn't gotten used to it: She missed him.

I'll fix that! She jumped up, hurried into the house, found the scrap of paper on which O.J. had written Denny's phone number in New York, and—a little embarrassed at bothering Guy—jogged a mile down the road in the dark to a pay phone.

"I want to make a collect call," she told the operator.

A minute later the phone was ringing. She heard a *click* and a voice said, "This is Denny. I can't come to the phone right now—"

The operator cut him off. "Sorry. No one there."

"Hey—wait!"

"If you want to leave a message, deposit one dollar and eighty cents for the first minute."

"But . . . okay . . . never mind." The line went dead. "It's no big deal." Lily kicked a stone and turned for home.

4 · *Sunday—New Arrivals*

≈≈≈≈≈≈≈≈≈≈≈≈≈≈≈≈≈≈≈≈≈≈≈≈≈≈≈≈

By late the following morning, Lily had already been in the studio for two hours, struggling with the oil painting. She had abandoned the sky—it seemed a mistake to have tried to paint it so fast—and now was working on the water.

It was better, but not like O.J.'s. His water seemed to ripple with motion, to swirl with currents. Peering closely, she saw that he had done it with lots of small, separate strokes and small differences in color.

Hmm. Lily felt a flicker of interest. How's he do that?

She'd awakened thinking about the painting, but putting ideas into practice wasn't that easy.

Frustrated, Lily put down her brush, padded to the kitchen in her bare feet, and drank some milk right out of the container. Then, she couldn't help grinning as she remembered how she always yelled at her father when he did that.

Lily was getting used to the silence in the cottage. It didn't nudge her painfully anymore. For periods of time she almost forgot that her father was gone.

There was a whole day ahead and she planned to fill it up with landmarks: paint, lunch, swim—maybe with Guy. She didn't think she could ask Anna Herbert again. Even though the lady didn't act like a college professor, the idea made Lily nervous.

She went to the doorway and watched the sea: all in one place, so full of movement. Cocking her head at an angle, she imagined the sand, water, and sky in three triangular shapes, one above the other.

Wish I could paint that.

She caught her breath. Why not?

The image stayed in her mind. Carefully, as if afraid to jostle it, she went back to the studio, ignoring the easel.

Acrylics, she thought.

She dumped out the paint box, separated the colors. There weren't many tubes of acrylic, but she found cerulean blue, which would do for the sky, ultramarine blue that would be perfect for water, and yellow ocher for the sand. They'll work, she decided. Anyway, it was the shape, not colors, she had in mind.

Her father had prepared a number of canvases—it was part of his process of "getting ready to make art." Lily picked a small one and stared at it for a minute. Then with a pencil, she drew a faint diagonal line, slanting down from left to right. Quickly she made another, coming from high on the right to meet the first line a couple of inches in from the edge.

The canvas was now blocked off into three sections: The one for the sand formed a sloping base; above it, the sea would made a perfect triangle; the sky was wedge-shaped, impossibly lower on the left than on the right.

Hmm.

Lily squeezed out paint and stroked on color: sand; aqua water; deep, dark sky. She made repetitive patterns and used a clean brush for each section—it was faster that way.

Finally she stepped back. The new picture made her smile. It probably wasn't a real painting, but it was just as much sky-sea-sand as any of O.J.'s.

Goofy, she pronounced it. A goofy Lily painting.

She placed it against the wall. In an odd way, it pleased her. She ate a sandwich, did push-ups on the deck, and was ready to face the oil again.

Squishing some white with the blue, she started on another corner. The paint seemed uncooperative; it smelled strong. The water she'd painted this morning was definitely better than the sky she'd painted last night. That was sort of hopeful, she guessed. But it resembled water only if she squinted and used a lot of imagination.

Biting the end of her brush, she heard someone yell,

"Wa-hoo! Look here!" It took a minute for the noise to sink in. Lily thought, Someone's out there, and went to the window.

On the beach beyond Guy's cottage, three people were standing in the shallows, whooping at the ocean.

Who are they? Lily wondered as she went out onto the deck. There were two teenagers, girl and boy, and a littler boy. The girl saw Lily, waved and gestured, then stood waiting, hands on her hips.

Hmm, Lily thought. Kids . . . go see.

She crossed the sand. The three of them stood in a row watching her.

"We're the Blakes," said the girl when Lily reached them. "That's our father's—" She pointed to the big house one up from Guy's. It stood above the dune with two stories rather than the usual one and a high deck surrounding the second floor. It was new and much more elegant than most of the houses strung along the beach.

The girl continued, "I'm Claire, fourteen. That's Graham, thirteen, and Joey."

Joey blinked and smiled shyly. "Eight."

"How d'ya do?" said Lily. "Lily Maxwell, ah, thirteen."

Claire smiled. She was a bit taller than Lily, sleek and tanned, with a black-and-white-striped bikini that she filled up on top. Lily tugged at her bathing suit. She kept waiting for her own front to grow, and it had, some, this summer. But not like Claire's. Lily crossed her arms over her chest.

"I live over there." Lily gestured with her head.

Claire said, "In Pearl Phipps's place?"

"Yes, um, my father and I. You know Mrs. Phipps?"

The girl nodded, unconscious of Lily's interest. "She's a friend of ours."

Lily couldn't help herself. "A *friend*?"

"Sure." Claire gave Lily a squint-eyed look. "Why not? She lives here, knows everybody, tells funny stories. She's rich. Daddy likes her."

Graham had short brown hair and appraising eyes. "Wanna go swimming?" he asked.

Lily adjusted her bathing suit. She'd been wishing for kids—well, here they were. "Sure."

The tide was fairly high, covering dips in the sand that made steep drop-offs. The ocean was rough, with strong swirly undertows, but the Blakes didn't mind. Fearless, Claire and Graham stood in the most dangerous spot, their footing precarious, laughing with glee. Lily stayed slightly back, with Joey. Her shoulder was still sore from her dunking yesterday with Mrs. Herbert, and she had a strong respect for the ocean.

After awhile, a man came toward them in the water, dragging two blue-and-red rafts. Lily had seen him before.

"Daddy!" Joey exclaimed.

"That's our father," said Claire unnecessarily. "Owen G. Blake."

"He's a surgeon," added Graham. "The G. stands for Graham."

"Hmm," said Lily. She never announced her father's occupation along with his name and decided the Blakes were sort of . . . braggy.

"Hi, Daddy," Claire cried, splashing over to him. "This is Lily Maxwell. Wanna come swimming?"

Dr. Blake acknowledged Lily with a wink, then beamed at his daughter and shoved a raft toward her. "Here, princess."

"Watch this, Dad," Graham yelled. He dove through the surf and began swimming straight out to sea. Claire and Dr. Blake followed.

This left Lily and Joey alone. "He gets us for a week. Ten days, actually, counting half-days," said the boy, his eyes on his father and sister kicking out on the two rafts after Graham.

"Why aren't you in school?"

"We go to private school." The boy frowned fiercely and looked almost like he was going to cry. "It doesn't start yet."

"Oh." Watching Dr. Blake, Lily remembered the times earlier that summer when his house had sprouted open windows and bright flags flying on the decks. Dr. Blake and a tall, blond woman had appeared, taking brisk walks, lazy swims. They never stayed long.

"You don't live with him?" Lily continued. Joey turned and headed for shore, his face so unhappy that Lily followed.

"No. He lives with this other lady. We don't like her." He gazed out to sea again, scraping sand into a half-moon with his toe. "Last year I got to stay home with Momma. But we're all going to private school this year. Even me. Whether I want to or not."

Lily could see he didn't want to. "That's tough."

"I know. Claire's going to tell me all about it. She's been there." Joey didn't look reassured.

"Well . . . let's make a castle." Lily had become expert at building castles this summer.

Joey shook his head. "I'm too big."

"What?" Lily shoved his shoulder gently. "Nobody's too big for that. Come on." She pushed together a mound and started building a wall around it, packing the sand. After a minute Joey joined in. They scraped a moat around the outer wall and made an entry gate on the landward side for the tide.

"Neat," Joey said. "Wait—I'll get some cups and we'll make turrets." Concentrating, he finished, then sat back on his knees and nodded. "Will the water get it?"

"Might." Lily calculated. "High tide was at two yesterday. It'll be around three today. In an hour or so."

"I'm gonna watch." He looked out to sea. "Here comes Claire."

The girl surfed in, riding one raft with the other bumping along beside her. Dr. Blake and Graham were talking far out beyond the breakers.

When Claire stood, a second wave slammed into her back and knocked her down. She got up again and splashed through the water, frowning. "Nobody's made their beds yet. I'm making mine. Then we're going to town for groceries. Coming, Lily? Joey?" She dropped the rafts. One of them hit the castle and smashed a corner.

Joey bit his lip.

Lily glared and bent to mend the broken spot. "Not me, thanks." She was irritated. This girl seemed to think she owned the world.

"Okay. You come for dinner? We're having spaghetti."

"Um . . ." Lily thought of her empty house, her paintings, her secret. She had to be careful. "I have to . . . be home. Maybe tomorrow we could do something?"

"Sure. Tomorrow." Claire smiled. Her teeth were perfect, white and even. She looked like somebody in a magazine, her hair sleek and straight, as attractive wet as it had been dry. Lily touched her own mop of curls, springing imperfectly in every direction. Claire went on, "We can swim and sunbathe and play Frisbee and baseball. You'd like that?"

"Oh, yes." Lily loved baseball.

"Good. Come in the morning. Come on, Joey.

Bring the rafts." She turned toward the house.

Joey eyed the castle and said wishfully, "It'll still be here when we get back."

It won't, Lily thought, but she didn't say anything. Joey took the raft strings and without a backward glance, trudged after his sister.

Back home the cottage seemed snug and cheerful.

Kids, Lily thought. She'd been longing for friends a few days ago, but things were different now. Without O.J. to touch base with anytime during the day, everything had changed. She had to keep the cottage safe from prying eyes, to keep her secret. To keep on painting.

Sorting through her impressions of these new acquaintances, Lily thought, They seem fun, but kind of . . . pushy. And they know Mrs. Phipps. That's dangerous.

She went into the studio. The peace of mind that painting required had temporarily vanished. Lily blinked at her canvas, frowned, and went outside, hoping to see Guy. She lurked on the deck, watching his windows. When he didn't emerge, she went down to the beach instead and turned south, away from the Blakes'.

She sprinted, then jogged, then walked, cooling off from her run.

Someone appeared in the distance, and soon Lily realized it was her other neighbor, Anna Herbert.

"Hi," Lily said when the woman neared. She had her hands full. "What've you got?"

Mrs. Herbert showed her collection proudly: several small perfect shells, a slightly chipped sand dollar, some bits of coral.

"You don't look for shark's teeth?" Lily asked.

"I usually look for shells."

Drippy, Lily thought. She glanced back the way she had come. They were pretty far from home.

"Ready to turn around?" Mrs. Herbert asked.

"Um, okay," said Lily. In person, Mrs. Herbert didn't make Lily nervous; just the idea of her did.

They walked for a while, then Mrs. Herbert said, "Have you been here long?"

"All summer. My"—Lily tried to think of what she could and couldn't say—"my father's an artist and he's been making paintings for Mrs. Pearl Phipps, who owns our cottage. You know her?"

"I think so. Always dressed like a gypsy and acts likes she's"—Mrs. Herbert stuck out her chin and proclaimed—"veddy im-POH-tant. That the one?"

Lily hadn't expected such an assessment. She giggled. "That's her."

"And your father's making paintings for her? I wouldn't think"—Mrs. Herbert searched for words—"it would be easy . . . pleasing her."

"You have no idea!" Lily blurted. "She—" Lily fell silent. Determined not to say too much, she bent

55

to pick up a smooth white stone, then rinsed her hands . . . and changed the subject. "Are you really a college professor?"

The lady smiled. "Who told you that?"

"Guy Franklin."

"The author." Nodding, she smiled as if she liked Guy just fine. "Well, he's right. I am."

"Why aren't you in school?"

"I'm on sabbatical. Supposed to be getting several years' research in order, writing some papers. I'll get to them in a day or so. I also wanted a sabbatical because I"—she looked up at the sky, kept walking, looking up—"I've been having some questions. Odd moments at the telescope. I—"

Mrs. Herbert bent to pick up a shell. Lily saw it had a hole in it. Holding it out, Mrs. Herbert said, "You could put this on a chain. Make a necklace."

Lily had made about twenty shell necklaces at the beginning of the summer. She'd outgrown them. "I'll try that," she said without enthusiasm. "Thanks."

They walked on, companionably silent. When they reached their own stretch of beach, Mrs. Herbert said, "Want to go swimming?"

Lily thought it over. Anna Herbert was okay. "Sure."

Guy was gone somewhere in the Maxwells' VW bus when Lily got home, but later that evening she found him sitting on his deck drinking coffee.

"Hi," she said. "Where were you today?"

"I was here, except for a trip to the store. I looked for you before I left, but you were gone."

"I've been in and out I guess. You must have stayed inside all day."

"Yes. I . . . got stuck on my chapter and"—he bent his head, then looked up from under his eyebrows as if feeling guilty—"took a nap. Sometimes it helps if I sleep. And it did. I was figuring a lot out, doing fine. Then the"—he pointed—"bellowing herds came."

"The Blakes? Did you hear them?"

"Indeed."

"Did they bother you?"

"They don't exactly make concentrating easier. Did you meet them?"

"Yes. They're kind of . . . full of energy, aren't they?" Lily was surprised at herself. Ordinarily this trait would have pleased her. "And they're friends with Mrs. Phipps."

"You'll have to be careful."

"I'm trying."

Guy scratched his head. "Well, don't worry too much. Mrs. Phipps is busy. I heard in town that some problems have developed with the new condominiums she's building. Maybe she won't come around."

That was good news to Lily. She'd made it through two full days without getting caught. Only five more to go.

Guy asked, "Did you have dinner?"

"Yep." She had eaten nothing but peanut butter sandwiches all day—six in all—and was pretty sure her stomach was getting glued together. "What did you have?"

"Liver."

"Liver?" Lily was glad she'd missed it.

Crossing the sand, she sat on Guy's deck for a while and watched the reflection of the sunset, which behind them to the west.

When it got dark, she said good-night and went home. Guy's typewriter started, making a dull vibration that carried across the distance. Lily picked up his book and started to read.

It gave her an odd feeling, as if she were reading the book right while it was being written. It was like plucking warm, fragrant candy from an assembly line long before it was wrapped and packed and sent off in trucks to the stores. Guy's book was good.

5 · *Monday Morning*

The sun woke her. Lily stretched, wiggled her toes. She was wide awake, full of energy. Couldn't sleep another minute.

Wonder what Daddy's doing, she asked herself. Probably sleeping. Well, not me!

She jumped from bed, got into her swimming suit, ate two stale oatmeal cookies, and went out to the deck.

The world was crisp and light. There were a few fishermen up and down the beach, many birds feeding in the swash when the waves receded, no one else around. Guy's curtains and doors were closed; so were the Blakes'. Lily grabbed a towel (damp because she hadn't exactly hung it up straight) and walked down the steps, turning south toward Mrs. Herbert's.

That cottage seemed asleep, too. Lily dropped her towel, raised her arms, and spun slowly, letting the sun and wind touch her on all sides. There was no one around, anywhere.

Suddenly incredibly lonely, she went into the water, plopped down where the waves could wash over her legs, and pushed her hands into the wet sand.

The water blinked and glittered. It went far, far away.

I wish Dad had called yesterday. If he were here, what would we be doing? Still sleeping. I slept later then. Next we'd get up. He'd make eggs and toast. We'd talk about . . .

She couldn't remember what they would talk about. Just anything, everything. Punctuated with silence comfortable as an old coat.

There was no talk now. Lily thought, I've probably forgotten how to chitchat with people! And silence . . . wasn't comfortable. It roared in her ears like the ocean.

Stop feeling sorry for yourself, she demanded. But she couldn't help it. This morning's loneliness had taken her by surprise.

Sand was working its way into the bottom of Lily's bathing suit. She ignored it, scooped up handfuls, and covered the tops of her knees, then stared out at the water, immobilized.

"Hello." A voice behind her made Lily jump. It was Mrs. Herbert. "Out early?"

Scrambling to her feet, Lily got more sand all over herself. "Hi. Yeah, I, ah, woke up."

The woman was wearing a straw hat and a big loose

blouse over a bathing suit. "I'm going for a walk. Care to join me?"

Lily almost said, You don't have to feel sorry for me! Then she realized that Mrs. Herbert didn't know anything about her, didn't know there was anything to be sorry about. Wading deeper, Lily swished off some of the sand. "Okay."

They walked to the abandoned fishing pier and back. Mrs. Herbert didn't ask any nosy questions, and Lily appreciated that. Chitchat didn't seem to be a problem. Lily paid attention and noticed that they'd walk, then have a little burst of conversation about the weather, the shrimp boat trolling out in the water, the fisherman who landed a small flounder as they watched. Then they'd fall silent and walk again.

Close to home, Mrs. Herbert gestured toward the row of cottages and said, "Whenever I come here, I feel lucky. The beachfront is so fragile. One day natural erosion—or a big storm—is certain to wash it all away."

"Really?" said Lily. "That would be terrible."

"For houses and people, yes. But beaches are always shifting"—for the first time, Mrs. Herbert sounded like a college professor—"there's nothing stationary about sand."

"Does Mrs. Phipps know that?"

Anna Herbert smiled. "Builders try to ignore science."

They fell silent again. Self-conscious and unexpectedly embarrassed, Lily began bouncing in place, ready to run. "That was a nice walk. See you later," she said, and took off.

"Bye," she heard Mrs. Herbert say. Lily sprinted into the water, smacking down her feet, sending up a spray. She turned and waved—Mrs. Herbert was smiling at her—and unable to stop running, dashed to her cottage and up the stairs.

Rinsing her feet at the faucet, Lily caught her breath. She could see Mrs. Herbert down on the beach sitting (on Lily's towel) and looking out at the water.

Not feeling lonely anymore, Lily wondered, Something about that woman makes me feel spooky. What is it? Slowly she realized: She's my mother's age. She's as old as Flora.

Well, she's . . . different.

Lily hadn't spent a lot of time with grown-up women. They'd been around, of course—an occasional girlfriend of O.J.'s (it never worked out), teachers, the mothers of friends. There had been a librarian she'd admired once, and female sculptors and poets and short story writers at the colony.

But there'd always been a bit of a distance between them and Lily. She had liked it that way. Felt safer.

Lily watched Mrs. Herbert gazing at the water, and thought, She's not too scary. She's not Flora. She's . . . sort of nice.

The woman moved and Lily ducked out of sight.

62

What I should do is . . . get to work, Lily told herself. She went into the studio. Bright and clear as if someone else had made it, the goofy painting she'd done in acrylics sat under the window.

Lily wrinkled her nose at the new canvas. It was just play, not the real art she meant to try. She went to the easel, stood uncomfortably before her oil painting, studying it with a cool eye.

It was disgusting.

The sky at the top was incredibly stupid looking. The water in the middle had one or two nice swirly places. The rest were murky blobs, or unfinished. The sand at the bottom wasn't even started.

See if you can finish it, she told herself. Dad paints in layers, she recalled. She dotted the palette with fresh colors. At least I can do that. Get the underlayer on—instead of trying to get it all done right away.

She mixed turpentine with the paint so it wouldn't be so thick and brushed on medium blue where the water wasn't finished.

Don't think. Get the canvas covered.

She worked with concentration. In one or two places, again, the water looked almost right . . . if she squinted. Realizing she was going to mess it up if she did any more, Lily mixed some brown-gold for the sand and started on that. Her brush hadn't been quite clean, though, and the brown turned muddy fast.

Now you're ruining it. Wait awhile. Let it alone.

The clock said she'd been painting for two hours. Long enough, she told herself.

Back on the deck, Lily blinked at the bright, late morning. Next door Guy's typewriter sounded once *rat-tat-tat,* then stopped. At the Blakes' there were towels on the railings and a bright new umbrella catching the breeze.

Lily decided to see who she could find over there. She trailed down the steps and along the beach. Almost at once Graham came out. "Hi," he called from the deck. "Whatcha doin'?"

"Nothing."

"Want to go swimming?"

"Sure."

Lily glanced up at his house. She couldn't see anyone else there. She hitched up her bathing suit as Graham jogged to meet her. His hair was tousled as if he hadn't combed it yet. He had on purple swimming trunks, and his stomach caved in a little. He was almost as tall as Lily and . . . kind of cute, she thought.

He veered off toward the water. "Race you to the breakers!"

Lily took up the challenge. "Beat you!"

They ran through the soft sand and into the swirling surf. Graham was about five feet ahead of her until he got knee-deep, then the cold slowed him down. It slowed Lily, too. She dove under a cresting wave, then swam straight through the forming ones. When she lifted her head, Graham was there.

"Beat you," he said.

"Hmm," she acknowledged. "Barely."

He took a big mouthful of water, lay on his back, and blew it straight up like a whale spouting.

When Lily tried to imitate him, the water sprayed high then splashed in her eyes.

"If you aim forward, it doesn't get your face," Graham advised her.

They practiced being whales, then dolphins, leaping and surface-diving like the mammals that were sometimes offshore. Next came bodysurfing, handstands, and tag. Swimming with Graham was different than swimming with Mrs. Herbert. More fun but harder work.

Finally they started treading water to catch their breath.

Making conversation, Lily asked, "How long will you be here?"

"What's this? Monday?" Lily nodded. "We stay till a week from today. Then we get up early and Dad takes us straight to school. Our mother comes up separately with our stuff. We're not even going home again."

"Where's that?"

"What? Home? We live with Mom in Chapel Hill. But our dumb school's in Virginia."

"You've been there before?"

"Last year," he told her. "It's the pits."

"Hunh," said Lily.

"What about you? Where do you go to school?"

"Umm. I'm not sure yet. New York, maybe. Or . . . someplace."

"Not sure? Why not?"

Lily shrugged, not wanting to admit she had no fixed address. "I'm on vacation."

"Hmm." Graham looked around furtively. "You wanna get drunk?" he whispered.

"What?"

"I know where my dad keeps his scotch and vodka. We can take some, water the bottles. He never knows."

Lily shook her head. She'd tried drinking before at slumber parties with school friends (but she'd never told her father). She hadn't liked it much and had decided drinking was overrated. Besides, she had too much responsibility right now. "No," she said. "Thanks just the same."

All right for you, Graham's frown answered. "Okay. See you around, then." He took off straight for shore.

Lily reached down with her foot and realized with dismay that while they'd been talking they'd drifted far over their heads.

"Hey, come back," she cried, momentarily panicky.

"Chicken," Graham laughed, not stopping.

Help, she thought. Then: Okay. Take it easy. You

know what to do. The shore seemed far away. She waited, feeling which way the current was pulling (north and east, toward Spain). She knew the worst thing to do was try to fight it, so she chose an angle, north and west. After swimming steadily for a few minutes, she looked up. She was closer to shore, close almost to safety.

She noticed that Graham hadn't made as much progress. Indeed, he was farther out now than she was. "Wait for me!" he yelled.

"You all right?"

"Come back here!"

Once she was sure he wasn't drowning, Lily called, "Swim at an angle. Head for that yellow house." She pointed to a cottage some distance up the beach. "Don't fight the current. I'll watch you."

Lily saw him get his bearings and set off strongly. Then she took a breath and pulled into her own steady crawl. By the time she paused, the water was still over her head. Graham was nearby. Ignoring him, Lily swam, gaining slowly. When she could touch bottom, Lily checked Graham again, then kept on, churning through until she was waist-deep.

Soon, visibly shaken, Graham reached her. "Boy, that was scary," he gasped. Lily turned her back to him and waded to shore. The current had carried them many cottages north of the Blakes'. "Whatsa matter?" he called, following.

Lily put her hands on her hips. "What do you

think? I don't like being left in deep water. Do you?"

"I was kidding. I knew you'd be okay. Can't you take a joke?"

"You're a creep, Graham. I'm not swimming with you again."

"Huh?" he said, confused. Then, falling in step beside her, he murmured, "I'm sorry."

Lily scowled. How could I ever have thought he was cute? "Forget it. Just don't do it again. To anybody."

"Okay. Lily?" he whispered. "Don't mention what I said back there, will you?"

"About what? Drinking?" He nodded, and she thought, Boy, this kid wants it all, doesn't he? Everything his way.

Graham looked anxious. "Oh, okay," she relented, bending to pick up a bit of black shell that wasn't a shark's tooth.

"Thanks."

By now the rest of the Blakes were on the beach. Dr. Blake hailed Graham and Lily, "Hi, kids. Want to play ball?"

"Yes!" Graham clapped. "First batter!"

Lily was still scowling when Claire greeted her. "Morning. Will you play? We have a bat and gloves." Claire was wearing a shocking pink baseball cap. She rippled her elegant arms and shoulders like a slugger getting up to bat.

Lily shaded her eyes. Nothing was happening at her

cottage. There wasn't anything she was supposed to be doing, not really. She grinned. "Sure."

After awhile Dr. Blake's face was red from exertion. "That's it for me, guys," he said, panting. "I'll make lunch." Joey followed him, and Lily, Claire, and Graham swam to cool off, then collapsed on the beach.

"Ah," said Graham. "I could stay here a year."

"Me too," said Claire.

"Me three," said Lily, but reminded, checked on her cottage. It was peaceful and empty.

Claire covered herself with Bain de Soleil, hair and all, and offered the tube to Lily, who took some for her nose. The rest of her was too tanned for lotion to make any difference.

Arranging herself so she'd get the maximum from the rays, Claire lay with her chin up, eyes barely closed. Then Graham announced, "I'm going swimming again," grabbed a raft, and headed for the water.

Lily watched him plow through the breakers, climb on the raft, and begin paddling out. "He goes far." She didn't want to mention to Claire how he'd left her in deep water, or offered her Dr. Blake's liquor. But she couldn't help thinking about it.

Claire sat up. "Graham's excessive." She frowned at his bobbing form. "Always proving something. He offer you any of Owen's booze?"

"Owen?"

"Daddy." Ignoring Lily's silence, Claire added, "Well, he will." She flopped back down. "He's into being bad."

Lunch was sandwiches, peaches, and bottles of fruit juice, spread unceremoniously on an old tablecloth.

While they were eating, Dr. Blake said, "Tell me about yourself, Lily. Who are your parents? What do they do?"

"M-my father is an artist. Oliver John Maxwell."

"An artist?" Dr. Blake lowered his sandwich in mid-bite. "What kind?"

"A painter." She tried to think fast. "He's . . . making paintings for Mrs. Phipps. You know her, I think. She lives here? My dad's got a real funny schedule."

"*Pearl* Phipps?" Dr. Blake eyed Lily's cottage with interest. "I'd like to meet your father. When's he arou—"

To distract him, Lily interrupted, "My mother is an artist, too. A . . . a jewelry designer in Paris." She spoke loudly, drowning his voice. She hated telling about her mother.

"Oh?" He returned his gaze to Lily. "Not *Flora* Maxwell?"

Lily's heart sank. "Yeah. Why?"

"I know about her. I got a piece. Don't they sell it at Neiman-Marcus?" Uncomfortable, Lily nodded. "Bought it for . . . " He trailed off. "My colleague."

His children might have been turned to stone.

Lily remembered: that tall woman. She's not their mother. To fill the silence Lily said, "What kind of piece?"

"A . . . pin. A twisted shape with, ah"—he shifted, brushing invisible sand from his leg—"one jeweled eye."

"Sapphire," Lily said, thinking, Probably cost him three or four thousand. "She's been into sapphires for years."

"Do you have any?" Claire asked, her face pinched. "Of her pins or things?"

"No. They're too expensive." Lily jumped up, hot and agitated; she couldn't just sit and answer questions. Running into the ocean, she leaped under a wave and came up on the other side. After finding her feet again, she rubbed water on her arms and told herself, Relax. Settle down.

How awful that Mother should be so famous. What a disgusting coincidence. Well, she was in *Time* magazine. Twice. Still, you'd think way out here at the edge of the world you could get away from Flora Maxwell.

A big swell lifted her. Right behind it another curled. Lily dove through, went deeper, and floated on her back until she was calm.

Then she picked out a good wave and surfed in to where the sand bumped her stomach. When she rejoined the Blakes, they were pretending to be unconcerned, staring every which way, except Joey, who said, "Hi. Sit down. We're sorry."

"Me, too," said Lily, kneeling on a towel to wipe her face on a not-too-sandy corner. "I'm kind of touchy about my parents." It was the truth, though she didn't much like it.

Claire flashed a dagger at her father. "So are we."

"Ha-ha-ha." Dr. Blake's laugh sounded hollow. "Have another sandwich, Lily. You eat like you're starving."

Lily hesitated, glanced at her own house, and gasped. There was Mrs. Phipps, standing on the deck like some kind of monster lighthouse.

"Oh no." Lily stumbled to her feet. "I'll see you guys. Thanks for lunch."

She dashed across the sand and up the stairs. The door to the cottage stood open; Mrs. Phipps had been inside! When Lily paused to rinse her feet, the woman rattled her bracelets. Wearing a pure white dress, she was crisp and angry.

"Young lady," she demanded, "where is your father?"

6 · *"Just Till Thursday!"*

"He . . . he's . . ." Lily was breathless, her voice rasped.

"And what is that thing on the easel?"

My oil painting, Lily realized with dismay. She couldn't think. "My fa—, my fath—"

"It's appalling. What's happened to him? I'd say he's lost it, can't paint at all. But for that other one." She smiled. Lily stopped breathing as Mrs. Phipps went on. "It's unfinished but so interesting. Bold. I like it."

"Y-y-y-you?"

"Yes, me. What's wrong with you? Can't you talk?"

"Yes." Lily bent to the spigot and rewashed her feet, gathering her wits. "Yes," she repeated, pulling a cleanish towel from the line and wrapping it around her waist. "My father's . . . um, gone for a walk. He's had a setback. Because of what you said. He feels bad. Sort of an . . ."

"But—"

"Artist's block."

"I made him feel bad?"

"Of course. You said terrible things. Artists are sensitive."

"Well!" Mrs. Phipps shaded her eyes and glared at the beach. "I want to talk to him."

"No! It's . . . a long walk. He's thinking. Part of the . . . process." Lily trembled. She was sure her visitor knew the truth. She wasn't glib enough to think of any more lies.

Mrs. Phipps tapped a glossy red fingernail on her elbow. "He must do more. Get moving. *I want paintings.* At least that would make me happy."

"Happy?" Lily echoed.

"Yes." Mrs. Phipps peered up and down the beach. There were a few people, indistinguishable. "I'll just wait a few minutes for him. Do you have a glass of water?"

"Sure, yes, excuse me." Lily fled to the kitchen. When she returned, Mrs. Phipps was sitting in a deck chair, contemplating a list on a page in a blue leather notebook, and shaking her head. She gave a huge sigh, and Lily asked, "Is something wrong?"

"My dear, you have no idea." The woman winced. "I've got troubles everywhere. For one thing—" She stared at Lily. Lily returned her gaze, trying to appear trustworthy and sympathetic. It worked. Mrs. Phipps went on.

"My new condominiums. I have such plans. They will be beautiful. The building's only started, but I can see it already, all finished, in my mind. Except"— she gestured, bouncing air—"I've had to hire new engineers and . . . there's a problem. The foundation. These new men say we didn't go deep enough. We went as deep as we could, but . . . the base might be shifting."

"Shifting?"

Mrs. Phipps seemed concerned, older, nicer. "They say we've built too close to the sea. It's a beautiful location. . . ." Her face changed, became hard again. "Of course we went deep enough. We must have! It cost thousands. The building will be all right. It has to be."

Lily was aghast. "But what if it isn't?"

"Then I'll fix it. Some people wouldn't, but I will." Mrs. Phipps's voice was low and steady. "You know, girl, I was raised in Texas. There was land as far as you could see. None of it belonged to us." She held Lily with her eyes. "I vowed to get out of there. Vowed to do things right. It hasn't been easy."

I bet not, Lily thought, almost in admiration. "Will it cost lots to fix your building?"

"Yes." Mrs. Phipps looked miserable. Her fingers tightened; her notebook shuddered.

Lily couldn't think of anything to say. She watched Mrs. Phipps with her mouth open.

"So! It's Monday." Mrs. Phipps checked the beach

once more. "Tell your father that I want progress! Paintings." She waggled a finger. "No more artist's block. He has just till Thursday!"

"Thursday?"

"Of course. I gave him a week"—Mrs. Phipps counted on her fingers—"and it will be up on Thursday." She stood, put away her notebook, all business. "It was kind of me, generous, to give him an extra week. But there's a limit to my kindness. You tell him that."

"Thursday's a week?" Lily counted on her own fingers: From last Friday to Thursday did make seven days. "You don't skip a day?" Mrs. Phipps shook her head. She looked determined and suspicious. Lily thought, Thursday's not what Dad said. Is it? But it's right around the corner. How great. "I'll tell him," she assured Mrs. Phipps and gave her the biggest smile she could manage.

With a flash of skirt and legs, the lady was gone. Lily heard a car door slam, the motor start. She crept around the cottage to peek down the side stairs. The white Cadillac backed out onto the road and pulled away.

Gone. Thank goodness. Now what? From now on, keep the doors locked. Can't have her walking in, poking at things, searching for "Mr. Maxwell."

Lily went into the studio. What did she say? She liked the goofy one. Said it was . . . bold.

O.J.'s patron had propped that picture on a window ledge. Lily moved it to a safer place.

Mrs. Phipps . . . assumed Dad did it. Lily stepped back, squinched up her eyes. *She's* goofy.

And my oil. She was awfully rude about that.

Lily backed out of the studio, unable to think about art. The whole cottage seemed violated, unpleasant, as if Mrs. Phipps had breathed up the air and sent it back, different. Lily went from room to room, sniffing for traces of her. There weren't any that she could find for sure.

Uncomfortable, she locked up and went over to Guy's.

"Hi," she said when he answered the door. "Whatcha doing?"

"Come in." He stepped aside with a flourish. By the ocean window, the floor around his desk was covered with crumpled papers.

"Troubles?" Lily asked.

"I'm stuck. Just can't seem to . . . get it." He rubbed his eyes, scooped up the litter, and stuffed it into a wastebasket. "Actually it'd do me good to take a break. Want to go somewhere? Get a hamburger?"

"Sure," said Lily. It wasn't that long since lunch with the Blakes, but she could eat again.

On the way out, Guy asked, "What's happening? Anything?"

"Um, well, Mrs. Phipps came."

"She did?"

"And she got in." Lily thought of the paintings and suddenly wanted Guy's opinion. "Could you come over a minute? I want to show you something."

They crossed the dune and Lily unlocked the cottage. Then she stopped at the studio door to bar the way until she could prepare him. "You remember that I was making paintings?"

"Hmm?" Curious, he peered around her.

"I've been trying to make an oil like Dad's dumb-and-ugly. Only I got frustrated. It's slow and hard. So real fast I made this other one and"—she moved so he could get by—"Mrs. Phipps liked it."

Guy went in. Now Lily knew exactly how her father felt, not wanting people to look at his work uninvited. Even invited it was hard. She sat on a chair, sat on her hands, bit her lip.

He turned to her and smiled. "I like it, too."

Lily protested, "But it's goofy."

"Not really. It's interesting, all of a piece. Good composition. Vital. You really . . . caught the sea."

"But—"

"You say you did it quickly, after working hard on the other?" Lily nodded. "It's the unconscious mind. Many people—artists, writers, scientists—have commented on it."

"How do you mean?"

"The human mind is deep, with many underlayers. What's on top, the conscious part—what you know

78

right now—is only the tip of the iceberg."

"Huh?" Lily knew about icebergs. The rest she wasn't sure she followed.

"The unconscious contains everything you've ever done, read, heard, felt. When you stop working, it keeps on. I know it's true for me," he continued. "I can be working on something, getting muddled, then unexpectedly—usually after sleeping—the answer pops up."

"Bursts out." It had been like that.

"Yes. Like a gift."

"I . . . don't know if I could do another." She wanted to ask what he thought about the oil and tried to hint, "Of course, it's only acrylic. Real artists work in oil."

"What makes you think that? Plenty of 'real' artists use acrylics. Like it better."

"Oh? Dad doesn't." She plunged ahead and pointed at her other painting. "What do you think about that?"

He glanced, spread his hands. "Looks like a struggle."

"It is. I'd . . . really like to start another. I'm kind of messing this one up."

He examined it more closely. "But there are places where you're getting it."

"Mmm." Lily was glad he'd noticed them.

"Keep it up. The two go together. This"—the oil painting—"is where you learn and grow. The other is like lightning. Accept it, rejoice, but don't count on it."

Embarrassed at being talked to so seriously, Lily said, "Okay. Thanks. Ready?" Closing the door to the studio, she added, "Guy? This doesn't . . . solve Mrs. Phipps. She wants paintings. In a hurry."

"Is that what she said?"

"She expects them. I'm going to keep the door locked, keep her out. But even if Dad brings pots of money—"

Guy shook his head. "What a dreamer you are."

"She wants paintings."

"Chin up." Guy shoved her shoulder playfully. "I'm starving."

Lily and Guy piled into O.J.'s VW bus and drove south to the small village where shops and the post office were. They ate hamburgers, milk shakes, and fried cheese at the Beach Shop, then drove down to the island's southern end, where they walked all the way around the tip. Not ready to go home, they got back in the car and sped twenty-six miles to the north end, singing along, at the tops of their lungs, with a golden oldies Beatles tape.

On the way, Lily saw a half-constructed building, tall, with open floors that the sky showed through. She wondered if that was Mrs. Phipps's new place. It didn't seem saggy in the middle. But who knew?

When they got home, the sky was darkening. There

were rain clouds to the south and west. Lily thanked Guy, then said, "Are you unstuck now?"

"Maybe." He frowned toward his house and desk. "I'll see."

Lily went into her own cottage and locked the doors in case Mrs. Phipps returned. The studio seemed welcoming and full of promise once again. Lily put the abstract where it wouldn't distract her and faced the oil. She decided to finish it tonight so she could start a new one tomorrow.

This time she made the sand a lighter color, lighter even than what O.J.'s instructions said. She thought about how the beach really looked: with little crab holes, differences in color, footprints. Wind-made knobs. Those things were too close up, like a photograph. But the differences in color . . .

She worked until dark, turned on the lights, and worked some more.

When she stepped back, it was finished. She didn't need to spend hours deciding, as her father did. He must like them, she thought, to stand and stare so long. I couldn't bear to.

There were a couple of places where the sand was okay. A couple of nice bits of water. Nothing was nice about the sky. Lily propped the canvas against the wall and made sure all the brushes were soaking in turpentine.

The painting was murky and full of failings, but it

pleased her. She was getting glimmers of what it would be like to make something that looked the way she saw it, to be able to catch the sea.

Already she understood more than when she'd started.

Lily didn't know for sure if she had any talent or would want to be an artist. But she wanted to try again.

Restless after so much standing still, Lily ranged through the cottage. There was nothing to do. It was too dark to run on the beach; she wasn't hungry, couldn't stand the thought of TV, didn't want to read Guy's book. She thought about going to visit one of the neighbors but dismissed them all. She didn't want to see anyone.

Except—

I'll call Dad. She got a handful of change and went out to the road.

A wind had come up, moisture-laden: Rain was coming closer.

I like storms at the beach, Lily thought, and jogged to the pay phone. She deposited some quarters and a nickel.

The recording started. Lily listened to Denny's speech. Then, to her surprise, O.J.'s voice came on: "Hello. This is O.J. Maxwell. If the caller is Lily— Hi, honey! I've been so busy, when I think to call, it's always midnight. I love you. Leave a message."

All messages had fled from her mind. "Yes, hi, it's me. We're fine here. It looks like rain. . . .

"Um, Mrs. Phipps came today. She wants you here by Thursday and no later. That'll be okay, won't it? Otherwise everything's okay. . . ." Lily had thought she'd tell him about her painting but found she couldn't. It was too new and fragile. The seconds were slipping away. "That's all, I guess. I miss you. Call?" She trailed off—hating answering machines—and finished lamely, "Bye!"

A few big drops splotted on the road. Lily raced them home. Once there, she stood on the deck a minute, watching for lightning, getting wet, thinking about Mrs. Phipps. Just till Thursday. Will I make it? Well, I took care of her good today. By Thursday Dad will be here. . . .

Next door Guy's typewriter was clattering again. Lily grinned across the darkness. Unstuck.

7 · *Tuesday—A Minute for Flora*

～～～～～～～～～～～～～～～～～～～～

Rain came in the night: suddenly, a downpour.

Lily woke up. A shutter was banging; the wind beat against her window, seeming to search for a way in. On the road a car sprayed by. Deep puddles already.

Wondering what time it was, Lily got up and padded to the kitchen to peer at the clock on the stove. The light made her blink. Three A.M.

Outside, the wind whistled. Lightning flashed. The ocean sounded louder, bigger. Lily ran swiftly back to bed and pulled the covers high. She wasn't really frightened anymore, being alone in the cottage, she guessed. Or . . . just a little.

Tuesday morning was cold and dark. Lily rose later than usual, but even so, there was no one on the beach. The rain made swimming impossible. She stood on the deck a minute, getting wet in her pajamas.

The water was dark, dark gray. The sky was gray, too, but lighter. Far off on the horizon, only one spot was bright.

Wouldn't want to have to paint that, Lily thought.

She made some tea, moving slowly, her mind on the studio. Then, still in her damp pajamas, she took a new canvas and stared at it as O.J. used to do.

Okay, get moving, she decided. O.J.'s painting seemed to be smiling smugly, while her oil, against the wall behind her, whimpered: Not good, not good.

It doesn't have to be good. I'm just . . . trying.

Before self-doubt could paralyze her, Lily grabbed a tube of paint (green), threw it back, rummaged through the oils, picked pink, mixed it with white, measured the distance from the top of O.J.'s picture to the horizon—one hand span—and the same distance down, drew a thin pink line across the new canvas. It looked like a tightrope, and she brushed, making it fuzzy.

She paused and tried to remember how her father began. In a corner? In the middle?

With the horizon line.

Then what?

Lily studied the canvas, trying to imagine how it would look when it was done. What would she see first, like best?

The breakers.

After several inch-close looks at her father's breakers—they were blue-white, foamy, and wicked—

she chose a thin brush and painted lightly where her own surf would be, drawing it in. Then Lily decided to work up to that spot and switched to the sand.

She painted steadily for a while, interested in getting the beach right, edging toward the foamy water that she wasn't sure she could render.

When the brown sand was done (sort of) it made Lily think of a pair of hands holding the empty space above. She plopped her brush into the turpentine can, got dressed, ate some cereal, went back to the studio. Okay, she told herself, mixing white with blue. Ready or not . . .

Her breakers kept looking like marshmallow fluff. Her neck was getting stiff, but she kept on working until footsteps on the porch jolted her.

It was Claire, Graham, and Joey. "Hi, can we come in?" asked Claire, pushing into the living room when Lily opened the door.

"Um, yeah. What are you doing?" Lily hurried to shut the studio door, glad O.J.'s was already closed.

"There's nothing to do," said Claire.

Graham added, "Can you believe we have only six more beach days and it's raining?" He flipped on the TV and flopped on the sofa, waiting for the set to warm up.

"So this is your house." Claire was taking everything in. "Belongs to Pearl Phipps. It's not that bad."

"No," said Lily, who liked it.

"She calls it the ramshackle place." Claire wandered from the living room, past the dining room table to the kitchen, running her finger on things as if checking for dust. Except she wasn't interested in dust. Clearly, she was bored. She eyed the door to O.J.'s bedroom. "Your father here?"

Lily contemplated lying but dismissed it as too dangerous. "No. He's out."

"Can we see one of his paintings?" asked Joey. Standing in the middle of the room, he was the only Blake who hadn't made himself at home.

"Yes!" Claire exclaimed. "He's not here. Let us."

"I can't take anyone into the studio." Lily tried to make it sound flatly impossible. "But . . . I'll bring one out."

"Neat-o," said Joey. Claire nodded and folded her arms. Lily darted into the studio, grabbed O.J.'s dumb-and-ugly painting, and propped it on a dining room chair like he always did.

"That's this beach," said Claire, adding as if surprised, "it's nice."

Graham glanced at the picture then back at the TV, where he had found cartoons.

Joey cocked his head to one side. "Your daddy did that? Wow."

"Your daddy cuts people open and fixes their insides," Claire reminded him sternly. "That's wow-y, too."

"I know." Joey put a finger in his mouth.

After Lily returned the painting to the studio and closed the door, wishing she had a key, she said, "Here, let's go to my room." Claire and Joey followed her in.

Joey sat stiffly on a chair and said, "We're having a party on Friday night. We came to invite you."

"A party?"

"We have one every year," he went on. "It's a tradition."

Frowning, Claire thumbed through a magazine she'd retrieved from under the bed. "Only usually there are more people to invite. Now there's hardly anyone good. Can you come?"

"I'm not sure. Thursday's kind of our deadline—" Only two more days! "If we're here, I'll come. Will Guy be invited, too?"

"Guy the gay? Of course Daddy'll ask him. He'll say, 'Busy writing,' but he'll come."

"Guy the *gay?*" Lily asked, irritated. Every time Claire opened her mouth, Lily liked her less.

"Yes, don't you think so? Always so . . . perfect. Always so busy."

Lily hadn't lived years and years in San Francisco for nothing. She tilted her head back so she could look down her nose. "I don't think you can tell by looking. And I don't think it matters."

"Well!" Claire flounced back on the bed and turned

the pages of the magazine. She came to a test: ARE YOU LOVEABLE? "Hmm. Got a pencil?"

"Sure." Lily found one on her dresser, then remembered her manners. "Are you thirsty? Like some juice or hot chocolate?"

Claire licked the top of the pencil and made a mark. "Yes, thank you. Hot chocolate."

Lily and Joey left Claire to her test-taking. In the living room, Graham was immersed in *WarZone* on TV. He said, "Chocolate? No thanks." Lily continued on to the kitchen, where she measured three cups of milk into a saucepan and dumped the contents of three packets of cocoa mix into mugs.

While they waited for the milk to boil, Joey said, "Guy saved Claire's life once."

"What? How?"

"Two summers ago, or . . . before that even. I'm not sure, but I remember what happened real good. She swam out far and got in trouble. Started drowning. Daddy wasn't watching; nobody was. Guy came shouting out of his house, but we didn't know why. He ran in the water and saved her."

"Then you'd think she'd like him."

"She did for a while. Talked about him all the time. But Graham says she overdid it. When we came back the next summer, she pretended to get hurt a lot so Guy'd have to rescue her again. Daddy yelled at her."

Lily shook her head and poured the milk. "Weird."

They carried the chocolate back to the bedroom. When Lily saw Claire standing at the dresser, a packet of letters in her hand, she almost dropped the mugs. My letters! "What are you doing?"

"What do you mean?" the girl asked sweetly, fingering the top of an envelope as if she were about to pull it out. It was green with bold black writing: from Flora Maxwell to her daughter.

Lily put the mugs on the bed and Joey hurried to steady them. Mad at herself for trembling, Lily ordered, "Give those here."

Claire waved the packet. "Why? Love letters?"

"How dare you?" Lily held out her hand. "Give them here."

"What if I don't?"

In the other room, the TV went off and Graham called, "See you guys. I'm going home."

Lily kept her hand out. She knew better than to try grabbing. "Would you really read someone else's private mail? If you would, you're a disgusting snoop." She kept her eyes on Claire and took one step.

Backing off, the other girl said, "All right. If you tell me whose they are. They've got foreign postage."

"Give."

Claire tossed the packet on the bed. "Oh, here. You're no fun."

There was a moment of absolute stillness. Then Lily scooped up the letters, dropped them in the drawer, and leaned against it, closing them inside.

Joey was still balancing the hot chocolate mugs on the bed. Claire looked baffled and expectant.

"Claire Blake, you're the most spoiled brat I ever met." Lily couldn't help it; the words burst out.

"Huh?"

"Yes! You think you can do anything and get away with it."

Claire stuttered, "N-no, I—" She grinned apologetically. "They're a big deal, huh?"

"Ohhh," Lily let out a breath, rubbed her hair, her anger punctured. "Not really. They're from my mother."

"Your mother? In Paris?" Lily nodded, and Claire rearranged herself on the bed, folding her hands, chastened and interested. "Is that just this year's letters?"

"The total. Fourteen." In thirteen years. "And postcards." She inclined a shoulder toward the drawer. "You missed those."

"What about you? You must send her thousands. I'd love to write 'Paris, France,' on my envelopes."

"No. I don't write to her. Hardly ever."

"But why? What's she like?"

Lily climbed onto the opposite end of the bed; Joey passed out the mugs of cool hot chocolate. "She—" Both the Blakes waited while Lily tried to answer. She didn't mind so much talking about Flora to other kids.

"She's . . . tall and beautiful and very busy. An artist." That stopped Lily. An artist. What makes me think that I—

Claire started to say something, but Lily lifted a finger to silence her. Then she couldn't think what to say and dropped her hand, sloshing some of the chocolate onto her leg. "That's all."

"Do you ever go see her?"

Forcing herself, Lily focused on Claire's question. "See her? There? Not for a long time. She's asked me, but . . . no."

"I'd *love* to go to Paris."

"Yeah. You're her type."

Claire frowned, ready to be offended.

"Um, well . . ." Claire wasn't that bad. Lily relented, relaxed, decided to tell the story. "When I went before, it seemed like all she wanted to do was show me off. She'd say, 'Isn't she cute? Listen to her speak French.'

"Only I wasn't cute. I was ten, always had a skinned knee, bruises, and bumps. I kept wrecking the 'frocks' she wanted to put me in, getting dirty. I couldn't learn French overnight. They talked so fast that it sounded like a jumble."

Joey's eyes were big. "Only ten?"

"Yep. She kept forgetting about me. Leaving me behind somewhere while she ran around the city." Joey moved closer to his sister. "That happened more than once. I learned to take taxis, to go places by myself. She'd laugh, say she lost track of time." Lily remembered her mother's words. "Said she was 'So sorry, my dear!' She was always nice for a while after that. But . . .

Flora friendly was almost worse than Flora critical."

"Like how?" asked Claire.

Lily thought back. "She'd either say something like 'Show off your chin; it's excellent.' "

Claire studied Lily's chin intently. "Or?"

"Or . . . she'd say, 'Stop smiling, don't be backward, what terrible manners.' " Lily grinned sheepishly. "Sometimes I did things I knew would make her mad just"—she remembered being fiercely stubborn—"you know, holding my own."

"You must like her a little. You keep her letters."

"No, I—well . . ." Lily couldn't explain that.

"Bad things happen to kids and that's the truth." Claire got off the bed and stood squarely in front of Lily. "I'm sorry. I shouldn't have gone in your drawers. Sometimes I'm just . . . thoughtless. Forgive me?"

She truly did look sorry. Lily said, "Sure, Claire. Come on," and headed for the living room.

"Why don't you come to our house?" asked Joey, following her. "We could play Monopoly or Parcheesi—"

"Or cards," Claire offered. "Poker? Have any money?"

Lily shrugged. What could she say? No, I'm penniless? "Not right now, thanks."

Claire noticed the empty sofa. "Where's Graham? He leave already?"

"Yes. Didn't you hear him?"

"No." Claire was ready to go at once. "Come on, Joey."

She's jealous if anybody's with her father, thought Lily, walking them to the door. If she weren't so dangerous, she'd be pitiful.

"Bye, Lily." Joey patted her arm.

Claire gave Lily a big hug, then held her at arm's length and said dramatically, "We children of broken homes have to stick together. You should work on her guilt. Get her to give you things. It's easy. I'll give you pointers."

When they were gone, Lily cleared away the hot chocolate, thinking, Flora Maxwell, guilty? Ha! Never happen. One of the mugs slipped from her fingers and crashed into the sink, breaking off the handle. Lily examined it in dismay: Mrs. Phipps'll be furious. She counted all the china and made a list. Maybe I can mend it.

Psssssh, I'm always in trouble.

After washing the dirty cups, Lily put the broken one on the table to think about later—maybe she could fix it with O.J.'s Superglue. Then she went out to the deck, shielding her head from the rain with her hands. The boards were slick with water, dark brown-gray, with puddles standing in every indentation. She felt unsettled, jangly. There was nothing to do.

Don't stand out in the rain, dummy.

Back inside the cottage in her father's bedroom, she

sat on the bed and gave herself a minute to think of
Flora.

Was what Claire had said true? That Lily . . . liked
her mother? She never thought of it that way . . . but
they were connected. Flora wrote, she called. In her
funny way, she seemed to care.

Even during that last visit.

Flora Maxwell had flown to America this past April
to make plans with Neiman-Marcus for selling her
jewelry. While so close, she'd come to see Lily and
O.J. in New England.

Lily remembered everything. She had stayed out of
school because her mother was coming and lingered
nervously all day in the front hallway of the colony's
huge manor house. When the car (a long limousine
with a uniformed driver) finally appeared, Lily was so
agitated she almost threw up.

Her mother was beautiful in mouse-colored slacks
and jacket, a sapphire blue blouse that sort of flowed
everywhere, her hair pulled tightly back, in her trade-
mark style. Her eyes were green like Lily's, only
darker; they were sometimes wide, sometimes slits,
always seeing everything.

Lily had refused to wear a dress even though—with
clean jeans and a "Save the Whales" T-shirt—she'd
known she wouldn't pass muster.

She didn't. O.J. didn't either. Although they had
nearly two hours until dinner, he refused to take his

ex-wife to his studio or show her any of his paintings. This made Flora so angry, Lily thought she would leave at once. Instead Flora proposed a walk through the gardens. Lily caught herself watching her mother with admiration. The woman moved with such sureness, boneless as a cat.

After cocktails and dinner, her face flushed from wine and compliments, Flora took Lily to a private den for a little mother-daughter talk.

"Well, you are taller. You seem older."

"I am older." It was three years since the disastrous summer visit to Paris. O.J. had promised Lily she'd never have to go back again. Not unless she wanted to.

Flora went on, "Yes, you actually seem to have some bearing. Odd, for one so young."

Lily didn't answer. Praise from her mother (if that was what it was) was even worse than criticism.

"Would you like to move to Paris?"

Lily stumbled. "What?"

"We could fix you up. There's something to work with now." She pulled Lily's hair back like her own. Lily shrugged and slumped to get out of her reach. Flora continued, "I'd like that. Put you in a really fine school. We'd have a . . . good time together."

Lily had felt panicky, frightened. To avoid answering, she asked, "What's happening in Paris?"

"The same." Flora pursed her lips as if saying *prunes*. "Work. Friends." Lily held her breath. She hated to hear her mother speak of lovers. "People come and go. I'm . . . tired of it."

You'd be tired of me in two minutes, Lily thought.

"So, what do you say?" Flora was smiling, misty-eyed.

"No, thank you, Mother. I don't want to. I'll stay with Dad."

Flora had flinched as if struck. She looked away with clenched lips and adjusted her cuffs.

That was that. Except Lily hadn't been able to forget her mother's face. So unhappy. It had never occurred to Lily that she could make Flora unhappy. It was always the other way around.

I could never live there, Lily thought, standing with a sigh and smoothing the bed.

What a ridiculous idea of Claire's, to make her feel guilty. I don't want anything from Mother. I just wish . . . thinking about her didn't make me so upset.

Funny how Guy said Daddy won't talk about her. I never noticed that. Thought it was only me.

The trouble was that Flora was gone but she wasn't. Even after all these years. She was Lily's mother, and nothing, no distance, could undo that. Even if they hardly knew each other. The woman kept on coming back, in her own way.

Lily went out on the deck, with her chin up and her mouth tight. The rain splashed her face.

Now there was art, complicating things.

If I paint, will I become like Flora?

Lily realized this was a question that had been in her mind for a long time. It hadn't been formed consciously, but it had stopped her.

No, I wouldn't be like Flora.

There are all kinds of artists.

Just like there are all kinds of people.

Lily watched the sea for a long time. She was getting wet. C'mon. Do some push-ups. Get your blood moving.

8 · Midnight Call

The rain kept Lily in the house for hours. She painted some more, getting the breakers almost right, getting the water . . . messed up. Disgruntled, she went to the window.

It was mid-afternoon. Still pouring.

There was paint all over her hands. She washed them, made a sandwich, read Guy's book, then stood in the doorway.

The rain was maybe a little less, and there hadn't been any lightning since last night. (Lightning was very dangerous on the beach, Lily knew. It could travel great distances across water, searching for anything upright.)

It's okay, Lily told herself—only wet—and got into her sweats and sneakers. Determined, she locked the door, hid the key under a shell on the deck, and set off jogging on the beach.

She went all the way to the abandoned pier, then

kept on, farther, farther, into the rhythm, her mind clear of all but running, not wanting to stop. Finally she slowed, exhausted, and collapsed on the sand, ignoring its wetness.

Goofus. Running in the rain, she scolded herself. But she was happy: her heart was beating fast, her limbs loose, the heat from her body meeting the wind.

Suddenly she stood and wrote in the sand where the waves would get it:

LILY MAXWELL WAS HERE

The tide was out now, and the storm had churned up the sea bottom. This was perfect fossil-hunting time. Turning toward home, Lily kept her eyes down and unexpectedly found the biggest shark's tooth she'd ever seen. It was two inches long, perfectly formed, all complete. Fantastic, she thought. Putting it in her pocket, she continued searching.

Nearing home, she saw someone coming toward her in a yellow slicker: Mrs. Herbert.

"Hi," called Lily. "Out walking?"

"Yes. I just"—the woman glanced back at her cottage—"couldn't stay in."

"Me neither. You should watch out for lightning, though. It's very dangerous on the beach."

Mrs. Herbert nodded. "I know. Thanks for the warning. You're soaked."

Lily touched her head. It dripped as if she'd been swimming. "We're at the beach. Supposed to get wet."

"Well, don't catch cold," the lady said, then waved her fingers and kept on.

Lily's own cottage appeared dark and gloomy. She took Guy's stairs instead. "Hi," she said when he answered the door. "Can I come in? Sit on your sofa for a while? I won't make any noise."

"Look at you!" Guy exclaimed. "What have you been doing?"

She hadn't even washed her feet. She was soaking wet and covered with sand. "Um . . . running."

"Can you go home and get changed?" She nodded, grinning. Guy was so . . . homey. "Then hurry back. I'll make you tea with honey."

"Okay." She took a shower while she was at it, leaving a swirl of sand in the bottom of the tub. Soon she was settled on Guy's sofa with the fragrant tea. He had twenty pages to type, he said, and she watched his back, lulled by the clackety-clack of the typewriter.

Guess I'm tired. Get things in perspective, she decided sleepily, scooting down and covering herself with Guy's orange-and-brown knitted afghan.

Finding perspective wasn't hard.

I can't wait for Dad to come. . . . That new painting is better than the first one. A little.

Lily snuggled farther, cozy and warm.

If I made paintings . . . they would be mine. . . .
Dad didn't want to show Flora his. Is he afraid of her,
too? . . . She's got too many opinions. . . .

"Lily?" Guy said. "Dinner's ready."

She opened her eyes. "I went to sleep." Feel like I've
been run over by a truck.

"Yes." Guy was peering at her with concern. "I
noticed."

"Hunnngh," she muttered and went to the bathroom. Her face was big-eyed and rumpled. Wake up,
she told herself.

They sat to eat. Guy said, "I got a lot done," and
fell to chatting only in snatches.

Lily thought, He's like Dad with a painting.
They're all nuts.

Pretty groggy herself, she ate and talked automati-
cally. About halfway through the crab curry, peas, and
rice, Lily's head cleared. She realized with a jolt, I hate
curry, but was too hungry to stop eating.

Next door there was a burst of laughter. Through
Guy's side window, Lily saw the Blakes' house aglow
with lights. A group of people stood on the upper
deck. "They've got company," she observed.

"A dinner party. Owen came over this afternoon to
invite me, but I begged off—busy writing."

"They're having a big party on Friday," she told
him.

"I know. I'll go to that one."

Another peal of laughter drew Lily to the window. The storm was passing. Puffy clouds raced across the sky, reflecting an orange sunset. One of the Blakes' guests waved her arms. She was wearing a black and yellow caftan and had a turban wrapped around her head. Lily gasped. "Mrs. Phipps!"

Hiding behind a curtain, Lily opened the window an inch. Mrs. Phipps was leaning against the corner of the Blakes' deck, talking to two men and three women. Her voice carried as she described her safari and how she stalked the poor rhinoceros.

She paused, and one of the men asked, "What's this I hear about your new condo building, Pearl? Trouble?"

The man was small and round. Mrs. Phipps glared down at him. "Don't believe everything you hear." Like a queen in trouble, she kept her head up, her back straight. Her glance moved quickly here and there . . . and landed on the Maxwells' cottage. "Have I told you about my protégé? Mr. Maxwell, the artist?"

Her companions shook their heads.

Mrs. Phipps leaned far over the rail, trying to see into Lily's windows. "Looks dark, but he might be there. It's almost time for him to turn his paintings over to me. They're going to be beautiful. They'll hang in my new building." She slung a quick smile toward the small round man. "Care to come see?"

"Oh yes! Let's!" said one of the women, and before

Lily knew it, the group had moved off the Blakes' deck and disappeared.

Guy was beside her. "Guy? They're going to my house. What should I do?"

"Did you lock the door?"

Lily thought. "Yes. I always do now. Should I go over there?"

"No." He held her arm. "You stay here."

Tensely, she and Guy moved from window to window, watching. The entourage crossed the lower deck, disappeared down the Blakes' steps, reappeared on Lily's. Then Pearl Phipps knocked at the door. "Yoohoo! Mr. Maxwell! Guess who's here!"

There was no answer.

She rattled the doorknob, then approached the studio window. "Ah. This is where he works. See the painting on the easel?"

Lily bit a knuckle. It's not facing out, is it? Oh please . . . She took hold of Guy's sleeve. He said, "Shh."

The woman knocked again. "It's dark in there. They seem to be away. Too bad."

"Maybe we can meet him later," a young woman in a pink strapless dress said. "Let's go now, shall we?"

"I brought him here," Mrs. Phipps bragged, leading the way. "He's up-and-coming. Hot in New York, they say."

"What's his name again?" asked the small round man.

"O. J. Maxwell."

"Never heard of him."

The visitors vanished down Lily's steps. The ocean drowned their words. She closed the window. "Oh, Guy. That was terrible."

Guy sank into an easy chair. "I was as scared as you were."

"Mrs. Phipps stomped around like she owned the place." Lily frowned at Guy. "Well, she does own it. She'll be back."

Guy looked worried. "I'm afraid you're right."

After Lily went home, her cottage seemed unsafe again.

If I'd been here, I'd have kept them out of the studio somehow. But we still only have one painting for her. She'd be so mad if she knew.

Mrs. Phipps was circling. It was harder than ever to keep her at bay.

Agitated, Lily paced the cottage.

It was too early for bed, impossible to sit down. Finally she put a lamp on the floor, pulled out the sofa—she liked cozy hiding places—and got behind it with a pillow and Guy's book. Here. Read. No one can see. . . .

The sheriffs and gunmen in the story seemed peaceful, their problems compelling, but . . . plain.

It was midnight when Guy roused her. "Lily?" he called, pounding at the door. "Come on. Your father's on the phone."

She'd fallen asleep behind the sofa. She stumbled up, dashed across the dune separating the two cottages, and leaped (sandy-footed) to the phone. "Daddy?"

"Hi, Lily. I'm sorry I missed you the other night. Sorry I haven't called until now. I miss you so."

"Oh, me too." Lily gulped and tried to wake up. At last, here was O.J. Everything was going to be all right. Lily felt herself relax with comfort. "You talk," she said.

"Me? Okay, ah, the show opens on Friday. They've already put ads in all the papers. The featured artists are going to be me and this woman who works in neon."

"Neat. I wish I could be there."

"There are a million problems. I'm trying to get all the paintings framed; some of them are pretty wet. Then I had to add notes and names to Andre's lists and send out more invitations. It's all hectic, but you know, nothing major. I miss you. How's it going? Everything working out?"

She didn't know where to begin. "Um, I guess. Mrs. Phipps is kind of a problem. She keeps coming around, looking for paintings. She expects you to be done with new ones and for us to be gone—by Thursday."

"Yes. I got your message. But . . . ah, Lily?" Lily's heart skipped as he went on. "You know how openings are. There'll be a big party, people I'm supposed to meet. Reporters, contacts. So . . . can you talk to her? Get us an extension?"

"What? Till when?"

"Till . . . Saturday?"

"Saturday?" All of a sudden Lily was wide awake. "What do you mean, Saturday? You're supposed to be here Thursday." He made a noise, but she didn't let him talk; she was getting mad. "And what about the paintings? She expects them. What about that?"

"Well, I—"

"All you care about is your work! You're selfish and terrible!"

"Lily, I just need you to—"

"I hate you!" She slammed down the phone.

Guy looked shocked. Lily felt her eyes fill with tears. She hiccuped loudly, ran home, and leaped into bed, weeping.

He's not coming.

I yelled at him. . . . She'd yelled at her father before, but never from such a distance or with such anger. She'd never said she hated him. She didn't hate him, but she couldn't take it back now.

Overwhelmed, she asked herself, How can I? Keep Mrs. Phipps away, get an extension . . .

Lily stared up at the darkness, weak and unable to move.

Another realization had taken the wind out of her.

His work. In its way, O.J.'s art was every bit as demanding as Flora's. He wasn't even thinking about Lily's troubles here, or about Mrs. Phipps, not really.

Meanwhile Lily wasn't supposed to worry about herself or school. She was supposed to take care of things, wait, be flexible. She was supposed to hold everything together, longer than she could, even past Thursday.

He's not coming.

Get an extension. How?

She was crying again and couldn't stop long enough to think.

Wednesday morning dawned clear, the air as crisp as if it had been washed. All traces of the storm were gone. Lily got into her swimming suit and went out to the deck.

She felt heavy, leaden, as if her bones were old, old. Having said "I hate you" was like a stone in her mind. She couldn't remove it, not yet. But some things were clear.

Of course O.J. had to stay for Friday night at the gallery. Lily had been to openings before; she knew how they were. She'd always liked watching the people and their clothes and examining the fancy food—it was usually too weird to eat. Openings were fun for the daughter, but they were work for the artist. Potential customers would want to meet him; everybody would have questions. He had to be there. And who else could ask Mrs. Phipps for an extension but Lily?

Having sorted these things out, Lily felt extremely guilty. She didn't want to think about her father anymore.

Out in the water someone was swimming. Mrs. Herbert. Without another thought, Lily locked up and dashed down to join her.

The woman said, "The rain stopped. Come on in."

"Okay." Lily laughed and jumped the waves, ignoring her worries.

When they were done swimming, Mrs. Herbert said, "Have you eaten? Want to have breakfast? I'll make some."

Lily decided it was still too early to do anything about getting an extension from Mrs. Phipps. She accepted.

They sat on Mrs. Herbert's deck, ate muffins with raspberry jam, and drank orange juice and coffee. Lily thought it was all delicious.

Afterward Mrs. Herbert held her coffee cup in both hands and smiled out at the water. "So, Lily. You seem subdued this morning."

"I'm all right."

"Trouble with your family?" the woman prodded, but in a voice that was adult rather than snoopy. "I never see them around."

"My . . . I live with just my father and he"—she heard herself continue as if from far away—"he's had to go away for a few days. I'm taking care of things." She looked right at Mrs. Herbert. "Um, that's a secret."

"From Mrs. Phipps?"

"Yes."

"And you're taking care of things? Must be difficult."

Lily changed the subject. "What about you? You have family?"

Mrs. Herbert's slight movement stilled. "Me? Not close. I . . . my husband died. Some years ago. We never had children. I have a brother on the West Coast, nieces, nephews. Our parents are dead."

It seemed a very sad story to Lily, but Mrs. Herbert didn't appear too unhappy. She went on, "I have friends at the university. And colleagues. Students. Wonderful students. I miss them."

"Mmm," said Lily, imagining college. It sounded very civilized.

"And of course I have my work," Mrs. Herbert continued. "Astronomy, the sky—they're endless."

"Do you look through a telescope?"

"We have an excellent thirty-two-inch reflector near campus. Good for teaching, some kinds of research. And I go to Mount Palomar, studying Saturn, unborn stars. Fascinating, very intense. When it's your scheduled time"—she was gazing up, her eyes shining— "you go before it's even dark—five, six in the evening. And stay right through till morning."

Lily thought it would be interesting to know so much about the sky. "All night? Don't you get uncomfortable or hungry or sleepy?"

"No. It's funny, but you don't. It's so wonderful to see things you've been reading and thinking about.

110

Much too exciting for sleep to interfere. When you get home, you have to figure out what you saw, bring back your data. A lot of it is on computer. Analyze, write it up." She frowned toward her door and shrugged. "Usually, it's no problem."

Lily didn't understand. "Usually?"

"I'll get to it. I'm temporarily unmotivated." She ducked her head shyly. "Maybe it's what they call a mid-life crisis. At school last semester, all I wanted was to be at our small observatory watching the sky for hours on end. Even here, with my unaided eye, I sit outside with the bugs at night and stare. The stars. I've studied them for years. Now, I just . . . like to look and think."

"You're stuck," said Lily, who knew about such things.

"For the moment."

"Will you get unstuck?"

"Oh yes. Eventually."

"I'm . . . having a kind of early-life crisis," Lily said. She wasn't sure what part of her troubles she wanted to explain. "I . . . kind of jumped into saying I'd stay here alone without thinking how. It's not as easy as it sounded."

"You leaped before you looked," Mrs. Herbert commented, and Lily laughed. What a funny idea. "And you have Pearl Phipps to contend with."

"Maybe she won't come today," Lily said hopefully. "Maybe I'll just wait until she does."

Mrs. Herbert bobbed her head in sympathy. "Good luck."

"Thanks." As if dismissed, Lily stood up. "Mrs. Herbert?"

"Call me Anna."

Lily didn't think she could do that. She blundered on. "Can I ask you a question?"

The woman nodded.

"I've been thinking about how people get wrapped up in their work. Like artists. Sometimes it seems their work becomes more important than anything."

She paused, and Mrs. Herbert said, "Academics can be like that, too."

"Is it bad?"

"It's life. The balance is what's elusive. Work, people, love. Remembering to pay the bills. Sometimes things slip away. One's chances. I was busy, but I would have loved to have had a child." Her eyes were warm on Lily. "A daughter like you."

Lily was embarrassed. She didn't know what to say. "Um, thanks." She had to get out of there. "Thanks for breakfast, um, Mrs., um." She bounced from one foot to the other. "I gotta get going now, okay? See you later."

Lily ran down to the beach and turned. Mrs. Herbert was watching her. Afraid she'd been rude, Lily stopped suddenly, cupped her hands, and yelled, "Did I hurt your feelings?"

"No," answered Mrs. Herbert, her hands cupped, too. "Did I upset you?"

"No!" Lily laughed and waved. She backed up until her feet touched the water, then turned cartwheels in the surf all the way to the front of her own house.

Then she stood, so quietly that sandpipers came close to feed at her feet.

What would it be like to be Anna Herbert's child? How sad for her never to have had any.

O.J.

Lily still wasn't ready to think about him. She moved, frightening the birds.

Flora. Did her chances slip away? Does she . . . care about us, me, after all?

Lily climbed the stairs. It was odd. She was alone but surrounded by ghosts. She didn't like feeling sorry for herself or being angry. Her parents were too complicated.

She was glad she was still a kid.

9 · *Wednesday—On Edge*

Back home, alone once more, Lily didn't know what to do with herself.

There were too many "Mrs." around: Mrs. Herbert, who was nice and unexpectedly becoming a friend; Mrs. Phipps, whom Lily was supposed to be doing something about; the former Mrs. Maxwell. . .

Lily found herself in her bedroom. She opened her drawer and took out Flora's letters. Lily rarely read them. They were full of opinions, long talk of successes and problems with work. But they also contained places where Flora talked about herself, tried to explain things. Lily had usually skipped over these sections as fast as she could. They were the scary parts.

Now she wondered, What all has Flora said? Would I be able to understand her if I tried?

A knock disturbed her. Lily froze. Oh no! Mrs. Phipps? Already?

She hid the letters under her pillow and peeked out the door. It was Guy.

"Hi," she said as she let him in, embarrassed to remember he'd seen her last night when she yelled at O.J.

He looked wary. "How are you?"

"All right, I guess." Lily rubbed her face.

"Are you sure?" She nodded, and Guy said, "O.J. called back."

"He did?"

"Yes. Right after you left. I told him you'd seemed fine before . . . that you were disappointed. He said he can't come now, and I said I'd try to help you. I came over when he hung up, but your lights were out. I guess you were asleep."

Lily hadn't heard him. "Thanks." She didn't want to admit she'd been crying.

"He shouldn't put so much on you."

"So much what?"

"Responsibility."

Surprised, Lily asked, "You're mad at him?"

"A little."

She shifted and frowned. "It isn't really like that."

"I know." Guy looked so anxious and nice that Lily gave him a quick smile. "You know, Lily"—Guy reached open hands toward her—"you can stay at my place. I have an extra room. So what if Mrs. P. finds out? You'll be safe. Let O.J. deal with her when he gets back."

"Oh Guy, thank you. But . . . no." It was good to have the offer of a haven, even if she didn't take him up on it. "What I'll do," she said slowly, thinking, "is . . . wait. She'll come. She'll find me. She's busy. Maybe she won't bother till Saturday. Meanwhile I'll be planning what to say. Okay? You think?"

Guy appeared dubious. "Maybe. Just remember that I'm here."

"I will. Thanks."

When he was gone, Lily locked the door. Then she returned to the bedroom and pulled out the packet of letters.

Ready? she asked herself, and answered out loud before she could change her mind, "Yes."

She put the envelopes in order, first to last.

The first had come when she was five. O.J. must have read it to her, but Lily couldn't remember his voice or how it happened that the letter was saved.

I saw a little girl in the park and thought it was you. She wore white woolly leggings and a red beret. I stared and stared. Of course, it wasn't you. She was very French. Her mother said she was five.

It did make me wish I could see you, little Lily.

I have found a way to form gold when it is very hot. It works well, but I keep burning my hands and also make many mistakes. Lucky one can melt gold and re-use it. I'm not rich enough to afford very much.

116

The next few letters, sent when Lily was six and seven, were filled with Flora's work, her opinions, and descriptions of life in Paris.

The French have constructed a new building for the arts and everyone is up in arms. I thought I, and my friends, would be the only ones to like it. But it turns out everyone does.

I've been here for seven years and my French is excellent, but the bookseller by the Seine still grumbles at my accent and the mistakes he claims I make. He saves me English-language novels when he finds them, and I go back, despite his gruffness.

When Lily was eight, Flora finally had enough time and money to come to America. Lily didn't remember much about the visit. Most of it had taken place in the park, and O.J. had invited two of Lily's friends to come along.

Even though I've often looked at other children in Paris over the years, I discovered in San Francisco that I hadn't imagined you. I'd wanted to take you to tea at one of the big hotels. O.J. insisted on the park, and actually, it was perfect to see you at play with your friends. (He can be right about some things.) You seemed unaware of my scrutiny. So natural, carefree.

San Francisco agrees with you.

Flora's next letters were filled with work and someone named Jacques, who went from indispensable, to
irritating, to "unmissed, I assure you," in the space of
three letters. Flora complained often about things she
didn't like: foolish fashions, boring films, "no music to
listen to at all anymore."

Then, before Lily's planned trip when she was ten:

> I'd hoped to have a wonderful new apartment
> and a nanny for you, but with the excitement of
> all these new jewelry orders, there's no time.
> We'll camp out in my hotel and have a wonder-
> ful visit. I can't wait.

When Lily returned to San Francisco, so happy to be
home, a letter had followed at once.

> I watched you leave today. You looked so
> young. I realized for the first time—Lily's brave
> to travel all this way alone. Although you
> didn't look frightened. You looked happy.
>
> After the plane's door closed, I couldn't go. I
> found a place where I could see the huge jet,
> and I stood, waiting. There seemed to be some
> delay, and I was on edge, wishing I could come
> and get on the plane, speak to you once more.
>
> I don't know how to talk to you. I never said
> I love you. But I do.
>
> It was too late for last-minute speeches. The

Air France rolled down to the runway, paused, took off. I watched the sky long after it was gone.

Then I found a taxi and headed back to town. On the way I suddenly called, "Stop!" The driver (grumbling) left me here, in a small cafe on the outskirts of Paris. The proprietor brought coffee, and now she sweeps the floor, eyeing me. Her customers don't usually arrive by cab, I suspect, or wear silk dresses and borrow sheets of paper.

I'm missing two important business meetings, but I had to write you before going back to my life. I'm sorry I was so busy these past days. Thank you for coming, Lily.

I feel so strange. As if I didn't see you until you were gone.

I wish she had come and gotten on the plane, Lily whispered to herself, her eyes filling with tears. Only . . . I was so glad to be leaving. I wouldn't have understood.

The second to the last letter was from this year. It was brief and full of plans again.

I will be coming to America in April and would be pleased to see you and your father. I hear good things about his work, was astonished to see his picture in the art journal.

I have been thinking of you much of late,

Lily my dear. You are unfinished to me, a question.

The last letter was brittle.

> My, how you've grown. I've been terribly busy. The Neiman-Marcus connection is excellent. They know what they're doing and their customers are grand.
> I'm going to an international gem fair. Thinking of changing to emeralds — they can be so clear.
> Do take care, Lily dear. Write?

Lily held the last letter for a minute, then put them all back in order, last on top, and tied them up again.

Flora never knew me. She could walk by me on the street and never know. She lost her chance.

Not wanting to think about her mother anymore, Lily tossed the letters into the drawer, closed it securely, and wandered back to the living room.

She'd told Guy she was just going to wait for Mrs. Phipps to find her, but waiting wasn't easy. She didn't feel like painting, didn't want to think about her father, had thought enough about her mother to last a week.

She went into the shower and stayed a long time, washed her hair three times, found some hand lotion and rubbed it all over her body, cut her toenails with her father's scissors from his paint box.

Then she sat down in the living room and picked up

Guy's book. She kept remembering, I should be planning what to say to Mrs. Phipps, but no plans came to mind. Reading took her away from the present, and that was fine.

Later that afternoon there were several people near the water in front of the Blakes' cottage. Lily locked the door, hid the key, as usual, under a shell, and headed toward them.

Dr. Blake sat under a large umbrella reading a book; Graham and Joey were playing catch; Claire was standing far up the beach, ankle deep in water, saying something and waving her arms.

"Hi," Lily greeted the boys. "What's Claire doing?"

"She's singing," Joey said. "She's begun doing it all the time now. Practicing for school."

Lily and the boys went swimming, and after awhile Claire came back down the beach and joined them in the water.

"How'd it go?" Graham asked.

"I'm getting worse," Claire said glumly.

"Worse at what?" Lily asked.

"I'm practicing a song. There's this girls' chorus at my school. Everybody important is in it, so I'm going to be, too. Except you have to audition. Last year I was too chicken to try. But this year—" she stopped, looking very determined.

"Can you sing?"

"Of course. Want to hear?"

Lily glanced at Graham and he made a terrible face. "She sounds like a barrel of trapped rats."

"Graham!" Claire squealed, splashing water at him. "Cut it out. I'm sensitive. Lily? Will you?"

"Okay." Claire picked a spot where no one— particularly Graham—was near, faced the ocean, and sang, "SomeWHERE o-ver the rainbow, WAYYYY up high. There's a—"

She kept on, holding her hands in a funny way, like an opera singer, and making trembly noises sometimes with her voice.

Lily liked "Over the Rainbow." O.J. often brought home VCR tapes with old Judy Garland movies (she was one of his favorites). But Claire didn't sound like Judy Garland.

"Well?" Claire demanded when she was finished.

Lily tried to be diplomatic. "Where'd you learn all that?"

"Daddy got me singing lessons with Madame Gra- zenspiel. From Vienna. Did you like it?"

"Um . . ." Lily wasn't going to pretend she'd liked Claire's singing when she really didn't. "I think I'd like it better without the Madame Grazenspiel parts. Did you ever see Judy Garland sing it?"

"No. Who's that?"

"An old-time singer my father likes. You can find her on tape." Claire looked so hurt that Lily offered, "Come on, let's go for a walk. We'll sing it together."

"Okay," said Claire, brightening a little.

Lily was surprised at herself; she was actually feeling sorry for Claire Blake. Claire soon recovered, and it was fun, walking along, kicking at the water, singing at the tops of their lungs. When Claire relaxed, her singing got better.

On the way back, Claire said, "Maybe I'll decide to be a concert star when I grow up. What do you think?"

Lily winced. "What are your other choices?"

Claire stuck her chin high in the air. "I plan to be a surgeon and a lawyer and an interior decorator . . . so I can fight my own lawsuits and fix up my own office."

"That's great." After a pause Lily said, "Um, Claire?"

"Hmm?"

"What's it like, seeing your father for a week a year?"

"Ten days," the girl corrected.

"Does it work out? Is it . . . I guess it's better than never seeing him."

Claire scowled. "I think if we saw each other for longer, we'd all kill each other. I mean—" She gazed toward her father's house which was coming into view. "It's so . . . intense. Getting used to each other for longer would be a lot harder. You'd forget who you really are. Don't you think?"

Exactly, Lily thought, but said, "Hmm."

They walked in silence for a while until Claire prodded, "What about you? What do *you* want to be?"

Lily shrugged and mentioned an old dream. "A ballplayer. Or an artist. Or . . ." She thought of Mrs. Herbert. "I might do something entirely different. Be an astronomer, maybe. A scientist. Find out stuff."

"Me, too," said Claire. "I'd like to win the Nobel Prize."

Lily, biting her lip, suppressed a smile. Claire was so competitive it was funny. "You could sing 'Over the Rainbow' for your acceptance speech."

By evening Lily's cottage seemed safe and cozy again. She knew she was only postponing the moment when she'd have to think about her father and deal with Mrs. Phipps. But for tonight she was happy to be alone. She remembered how nervous she'd been that first night, how she had jumped at the smallest sound. Now she couldn't imagine being afraid.

And all day Mrs. Phipps hadn't come.

Lily hummed, driving away worries. She was finally ready to paint again. She put blankets over the windows (Phipps-proofing the studio) and worked on her oil painting.

In the morning she thought, Thursday. Well, maybe Mrs. P. won't come today, either.

When Lily looked out the window, she saw that Anna Herbert was already in the water. Running to join her, Lily felt a little self-conscious after their talk yesterday. Perhaps Mrs. Herbert was self-conscious, too, for she kept looking down, her smile crooked. Then a big wave dunked them . . . and the ocean made everything all right.

Lily was practicing walking on her hands—hard to do for more than about ten seconds—when she heard Mrs. Herbert say, "Look! Who's that?"

When Lily surfaced, the professor was pointing toward Lily's house. "Mrs. Phipps!" Lily gasped. "Oh no!"

She fought her way out of the water, across the sand, up the stairs, to stand dripping before her visitor.

"Young lady, where is your father?"

"Oh, ah, ah," Lily panted. How could Mrs. P. be here so early? "He's uh . . ." She peeked under the house. The car was gone. Guy had said he would be using it to get typewriter cartridges and a ream of paper from Wilmington.

"He's gone. Gone to Wilmington." She caught her breath, washed her feet, pushed the hair out of her eyes.

"Eh? What for?"

"For? Supplies. You know, paint."

"Let me in, then. I'll wait."

Lily's heart was beating fast. She couldn't think, was afraid she'd let something slip or blurt out everything. Taking a deep breath, she pinched herself with her fingernails.

Oh God, forgive me for being such a liar. "I don't

have the key. I'm locked out." She tried to keep her eyes from the shell, three feet away, where the key was hidden. "By mistake."

"Well!" Mrs. Phipps glared at Lily. "How is the work coming?"

"Umm," Lily wobbled. Thinking, Get yourself together, she began, "My father is making wonderful paintings for you." She closed her mind to the fact that there was still only one inside. "You'll be very happy."

Mrs. Phipps smiled slightly. "Yes?"

"They're just . . . harder than he thought. Your criticism was very . . . useful. The new paintings—"

Impatient, Mrs. Phipps demanded, "I want to see them."

Lily faltered. "You can't."

Her opponent's eyes narrowed. "I most certainly can. I have a key to this house. I'll let myself in."

"No!"

Lily's outburst was so heartfelt that Mrs. Phipps gawked. "Why not?"

"You can't before he's ready!"

The lady sputtered. "B-but today's your deadline. Thursday. That's a week."

"Yes. That's another thing. It's taking longer. Because he's making paintings. Like you wanted. We need to stay till the weekend."

"What?" Mrs. Phipps came close to Lily and demanded, "What's going on here? I haven't seen hide nor hair of O. J. Maxwell all week."

"He—" Lily tried to smile in an encouraging manner. Now that the confrontation was actually happening, she felt better. Something had to work. "You'll be so proud. You really will." Mrs. Phipps appeared confused, and Lily pressed, "Don't you have other things to worry about?"

"Girl, you have no idea."

Lily stood firm. "We're the least of your troubles. Don't worry, okay? Truly."

Without speaking, the woman headed for the stairs by the side of the house. Lily followed. "Okay? Till the weekend?"

Mrs. Phipps swept downward. "No."

Lily pursued. "Huh?"

Mrs. Phipps stopped at her enormous white convertible. She looked angry. "I'm going to find my key. I want satisfaction. You'll be out of here by Saturday"—her face was red—"if I have to get my lawyers."

Lily leaped at that. "Till Saturday! That's all he needs. Everything'll be fine then. You'll see."

The lady got into her car and started the engine with a roar. "Fine? Ha! Nothing goes right!" She didn't wait for an answer. She drove away.

10 · *Thursday Painter*

≈≈≈≈≈≈≈≈≈≈≈≈≈≈≈≈≈≈≈≈≈

Lily held on to the side of the house long after Mrs. Phipps's car had disappeared.

Boy, she was mad. Did she say till Saturday? Yes, but . . .

Walking up to the deck, Lily's knees trembled. She sank into a chair. She'll be back. She's looking for her key. What all did I say? Paintings. Lily groaned. I said, He's making paintings. And, You'll be very proud.

Should I run to the phone, beg O.J. to drop everything and make some? No. Lily knew how the days before an opening were. He always had a million things to do.

That woman's gonna catch me. She'll find out. I wonder if big, important people can put kids in jail? Kids and their fathers—

"Lily!" Lily jumped. Who was that? "Over here! It's me, Anna."

Mrs. Herbert was leaning toward Lily from her deck three doors down. Lily leaned out over her own railing. "Hi."

"Was that Pearl Phipps?" Lily nodded. "How was it?"

The situation with Mrs. Phipps was too complicated to explain. Lily looked for a glimmer of hope and called across the distance, "She didn't find out." Yet.

"Good." Mrs. Herbert raised a fist as if Lily had announced a victory. "See you later." She went inside her cottage.

Lily drooped, then went indoors to the studio.

I don't think I should have said he was painting, Lily worried. I mean, what if she came in here? What would she see?

Lily's first oil painting was horrid and amateurish. The second was sort of finished. Lily had learned a lot on it, but nobody would call it "good." The sky, which she'd tried to do last night, had turned out murky, goopy, all wrong. Lily had expected that section to be the easiest, and instead, again, it was the hardest.

Lifting the picture from the easel, she put it against the wall, face in.

Paintings. The Phipps wants paintings. If she saw those two, she'd know something was wrong.

So what've we got? One dumb-and-ugly. One goofy Lily.

Lily glanced at that one. Mrs. Phipps had actually

liked it. Said it was . . . bold. Bold but unfinished.

Unfinished? How? Lily couldn't imagine. It wasn't signed, of course, and there were some wobbly spots, mistakes that showed up when you looked close. Was that what she meant?

Lily stepped back, all the way across the room.

I wonder.

She stood motionless, staring at her goofy abstract. I'll make another. One or two. Because . . . I'd like to.

And because . . . if Mrs. P. thinks O.J. did them, and just hates them in her regular way like she hated the others, then . . . maybe she won't find out he's been gone.

Standing in the middle of her father's studio, Lily decided something. She would never again—never in her whole life—put herself in the position where she had to lie like this. To live a lie. She didn't like it.

Pleased to have decided things, to be taking action, she put a new canvas on the easel, looked from it to the goofy and back. Couldn't help smiling. The goofy painting was different—free, happy, easy. She wiggled her fingers in anticipation and pored over the paint box, picking out all the acrylics and touching the colors.

I can add pink to the dark blue sky, she thought. Keep the ultramarine water the same—it's so bright and perfect and . . . try to get the ocher beach lighter somehow.

Gradually the echoing voices (her own, the angry woman's) faded away, and soon the world contained just Lily and the painting. She had some new ideas that had been lurking right below the surface of her mind. Filling each section with wavy strokes, she lost track of time. When she paused, she was amazed at how quickly the work was going and how satisfying it was. She felt as if she could paint forever—it was like flying.

Quick as that, it was done.

Lily put the new canvas beside the first. This one, too, had some wobbly spots, mistakes, but from halfway across the room, they disappeared. Grinning, she took another canvas, looked at it, and paused.

Couldn't stop smiling. On the next one . . .

She was full of commotion inside. Not ready to begin. Painting, she was discovering, could actually be wonderful.

Is this how Dad feels?

Suddenly she had to talk to him. I don't hate him. He must know that. But . . . I have to tell him. And tell him I got the extension, sort of.

And . . . connect.

She found change, jogged down the road, and dialed Denny's number. She hoped to talk to the recording; it would be easier that way. But O.J. himself answered. "Hello?"

Lily was so surprised that she almost hung up. She squeaked, "Dad?"

"Lily! Hi. How are you?"

She took a deep breath and pretended she was talking to the machine. "Hi. I don't hate you. I'm sorry. I got the extension from Mrs. Phipps."

He was excited. "You did? You don't? Oh Lily!"

She couldn't answer and there was a pause.

"Lily? I wish I could come today. Really. I know I make things hard for you. Sometimes I . . . I'm afraid I'm not as good a parent as you deserve."

He was sounding guilty and she couldn't stand it. "Cut it out."

"I mean it."

"You have big things to do sometimes. I understand that. They're important."

"Oh honey, my little green eyes." Now he sounded all lovey-dovey.

She toughened, even though she was very glad to be talking to him, to be hearing his voice. "I guess you're really busy, huh?"

"Incredibly. Some of the paintings are still a bit too wet. That's what we're doing now: trying to dry them with hair dryers. The frames aren't all finished. And—"

She cut him off. "I know. A million problems."

"At least." There was another pause. "Lily? Are you there? Tell me about Mrs. Phipps."

"She came and she's . . . mad, but I think she's giving us till Saturday. Only . . ."

"Yes?"

What could she tell him: I'm tired of lying? She

said she'll bring her lawyers? She's making up a bill? "She suspects. She wants paintings."

"I know. Don't worry, honey, okay? I'll take care of everything when I get there."

"Don't worry? How? I'm here."

"Do you want to go over to Guy's? He said you could."

"And hide? No." She looked across the road at a squatty cluster of apartments, her eyes filling with tears. He was far away and didn't understand what was happening here. "No," she repeated, her voice rising despite herself. "Forget it, Dad. I'll be okay."

"Lily? I love you."

She loved him, too. She knew she was important to him in one way and his work was important in another. Sometimes the work was big and consuming, but that was all right. They were in it together.

She could see him clearly, as if he were standing right there: his curly hair, his scruffy sweater, his million problems. She accepted all of it.

She whispered, "I love you, too, Dad. Bye!"

"Hey, wait!"

Her voice cracked. "Y-y-yes?"

He didn't sound so good, either. "Umm, nothing. I'll see you soon." They hung up; the connection ended.

Lily stood still, not crying exactly, but numb.

The sky was high and brilliant. A car passed, a bird called. Lily thought, I didn't tell him about my paintings. But—she started to jog—that's all right. What could I say? Move over, Rembrandt? Ha!

In the studio she took a new canvas, put it on the easel, lifted her shoulders, and blinked at the two goofy paintings.

She was making them for herself now. Dad said he'd take care of everything. Lily put up her chin. Well, maybe he can.

For the next one, she already had a plan.

Reverse the colors.

She'd make the sky pale ultramarine and pink (a sunset), the water deep blue, the sand—she didn't have many colors—ocher and black again . . . but darker . . . almost in shadow.

She'd been painting an hour or so when steps on the deck jolted her. She jumped, then was relieved to see the visitor was Joey. He looked as if he'd been crying. "Lily? Claire wants you. Can you come?"

"What's up? Hold on a second."

She ran into the studio, reached toward the new painting as if to say, *wait,* checked the tubes to be sure they were closed, and shoved the brushes into water. Then she hurried to shut the door and lock the front one securely.

Joey hadn't moved. "What's wrong?" Lily asked.

His chin quivered. "It's terrible. We—" He didn't finish. "Just come."

Lily followed him, thinking someone must have

gotten hurt, or maybe war was declared, or . . .

The other Blakes were sitting near the water. They didn't look tragic. A large yellow umbrella shaded the doctor. Graham sprawled beside him, half under the umbrella and half out. Claire was lying in the sun, glistening with suntan oil.

"Hi," Lily greeted them. "Something wrong?"

"Welcome," said Dr. Blake, although he didn't appear happy to see Joey with Lily in tow.

Graham didn't move, his face a mask. Claire sat up, thunderous. "We have to leave Saturday morning."

"We'll be at school two days early," Graham added, frowning at Lily as if he could bite her in half. "A real bummer."

"Is that all?" Lily asked, incredulous. Up against her imaginings, this seemed ludicrous.

"You don't understand," Claire spat. "Dad's a real turd."

"Claire!" Her father was shocked.

Lips tight, she said, "I'm sorry." She didn't sound sorry.

"Now kids," Dr. Blake began, his manner placating. "You know I can't help it. The school says you can come early. It's all set."

Joey said, "He promised we wouldn't have to."

"I told you. We tried, but they couldn't reschedule my surgeries. I have three on Monday morning. I have to get back, go over the records, visit the patients." He chuckled humorlessly. "You wouldn't want me to

135

take out Mrs. Jones's gall bladder and give Mr. Smith a hysterectomy, would you? Instead of vice versa?"

If it was a joke, none of his children laughed.

"That lady called," Joey told Lily.

"His girlfriend," Graham added in a mincing voice.

"Yes." Dr. Blake's tone was cold and deadly. "Dr. Dempsey is her name. You know that. Jealousy doesn't become any of you." He threw down his book. "You disappoint me." With that, he strode away up the beach.

His children watched. All three appeared lost and anxious. Joey had begun to sniffle. Graham lurched to his feet. "Hey Dad, wait. I'm sorry." He trotted after his father.

Claire turned away from them and glared at the ocean.

Lily asked Joey, "What's wrong? I mean, you knew you were going to have to go."

"On Monday. He promised. He promised he'd fix it so we'd have till Monday. And—"

"And what?" Lily prodded gently.

His voice was small. "I don't want to go to that school."

"Why?"

"Last year I got to stay home with Momma. I went to school by where she lives. I was happy."

"Oh, Joey." Claire scooted over to him. "Remember, we decided. Mom has to go back to college full-time. She needs to. You know that." Joey sniffed. "You agreed."

He stared hard at his feet. "You told me they make the little kids wear diapers. And get paddled."

"I was kidding."

"You told me."

Claire got on her knees in front of him. "Listen, Joe, I was just messing around. Scaring you, okay? They're great to kids there. You'll like it."

He wiped his nose with the back of his hand. "Yeah?"

She nodded.

"Will you watch out for me? Help me?"

"Yes."

"Promise?"

Claire eyed Lily as if recognizing a witness. "I promise."

Joey sniffed again and sat in his father's chair. "All the same, I miss Momma."

"I know." Claire looked bleak for an instant, then stood, brushing off her knees, and said to Lily, "Our mother is really a very nice woman. Boy, I'm mad at Dad. It's the principle. Come on, Lily. Let's swim." She ran into the water.

"Wait." Lily bent to Joey. "Are you all right?"

He compressed his lips. "I don't want to go."

"I know. But you'll be fine." She gave him a quick kiss on the cheek, surprised at herself. How many times had grown-ups said that to her? Did she believe them? "Come swim with us?"

"No." He was scraping sand together with his feet. "I'm okay."

Lily left him and waded out to Claire.

"I know we're ridiculous," said Claire, standing in the shallows with water almost up to her bathing suit bottom. "But we look forward to this trip all year. Then it's cut short. Ten days always seems like forever. But it isn't."

"It's hard for all of you," said Lily, bobbing her head in sympathy.

Claire splashed water on her arms. "Dad got me a tape of that Judy Garland person. I've been practicing. Want to hear?"

"Now? Sure."

She sang "Over the Rainbow" all the way through. Her eyes were big; she put more feeling behind the words. She looked nicer than usual. The song was simpler and better, and Lily realized Claire really could hit most of the notes right.

"Good," said Lily when Claire was done.

"Are you sure? Should I do any special things, you know, with my hands or anything? Like Madame taught me?"

"No. Nothing. Forget about being fancy. Just . . . think about how we stood here. Remember how the waves sparkled. Forget everything else and sing." Lily considered, then pronounced: "You'll make it."

Claire smoothed her hair and pulled at her bathing suit, showing a flash of white skin. Her tan was astonishing. "If I do, it's all because of you."

Lily bowed. "Me and Judy Garland," she said. "At your service."

When Graham and Dr. Blake returned, Claire said, "We're still having our party tomorrow night. Can you come over early, Lily? And help us? Please? Everything will be so beautiful. We'll put candles on the railings and make little tiny sandwiches and have a night to remember all year!"

Lily happened to catch the look that Dr. Blake gave his daughter just then. There was such love and sadness in his eyes that she had to look away.

At home Lily thought for a minute about the Blakes, how they seemed caught in patterns they couldn't change. She thought of her own conversation with her father. She felt closer to him but more separate; it was a new feeling. New, but good. In the studio, working hard on her third painting, Lily couldn't help humming. This can't really be work, she thought. It's fun.

When she was done, she put the new canvas beside the others. It was peculiar—lighter sky than water, spooky-looking sand. Different from the others, but it fit with them. Lily still liked the first one best.

All three did catch the sea, as Guy had said. Lily thought with a little shiver, I did that.

She decided to go tell Guy.

"Hi," he said when she knocked at his door. "I was wondering what you were doing."

The typewriter had been clattering all day. "Work going good?" Lily asked. "Can you stop for a minute?"

"Yep. What's up?"

She told him about Mrs. Phipps's visit and the extension and the call to O.J. Then she was too shy to mention her paintings.

He didn't notice her hesitancy. "Bravo!" he said. "I'm ready for a break. Want to go for a walk?"

"Okay, but . . . what if Mrs. Phipps comes back? She said she was looking for her key."

"She won't today. I heard at the post office that she's having a big meeting with all her engineers and about a hundred lawyers. Working out some problem."

"Her sinking condominiums." Lily was pleased. Maybe the woman's other troubles would make her forget the Maxwells.

Soon she and Guy were splashing along in the shallow water. Instead of searching for shark's teeth, Lily kept her eyes up, on the horizon, the shadings of the sea, the sky. After awhile she said, "Um, Guy?"

"Hmm?"

"Remember that painting I did? The abstract one?"

"I liked it. Like to see it again."

Lily ducked her head with pleasure. "Well, I . . . made two more."

"Really?"

"They just sort of popped out." She paused.

"You sure you're not an artist?"

Lily hugged herself, twirled away from him, stopped. "Now *that's* ridiculous." She couldn't hide her grin. "But it was fun."

11 · *Friday Night Gala*

≈≈≈≈≈≈≈≈≈≈≈≈≈≈≈≈≈≈≈≈≈≈≈≈≈≈≈≈≈≈

On Friday morning, as usual, the sun came in and woke Lily. She stretched, wiggled her toes, looked out the window.

Gonna be another perfect day.

She sank back onto her pillows. Could be my last one.

O.J. had called Guy's last night. He'd told Lily he was almost through with his million things to do. The opening would be tonight, and he'd said he'd call when it was over and then start out for North Carolina.

He shouldn't drive all night like that, Lily thought, anxious despite his promises to pull over and sleep if he got tired.

I'll be glad to see him. But—

The things she'd been thinking about and doing this week weren't quite settled.

Flora. Since reading her mother's letters—and since

getting to know Anna Herbert, and even Pearl Phipps—it was as if Flora Maxwell had lost some of her frightful power.

And painting.

It had been hard work and then such an unexpected pleasure. Lily got up and padded into the studio.

The new paintings were still goofy. She was sorry about the wobbly spots, but she knew that trying to paint over them would just make things worse.

They're good enough for me, Lily thought. As for Mrs. Phipps, Lily was tired of worrying about her.

She got dressed, ate breakfast, and went down to the beach. Mrs. Herbert wasn't there. Lily stood in the water a minute, staring at the professor's house. She wasn't in the mood to be frustrated, so she walked up and knocked at the door. "Hi," she said when the woman answered. "Want to go swimming?"

Mrs. Herbert was still in her nightgown, her reddish hair rumpled. "Sure," she said. "Good morning. Um, just a minute."

"Did I wake you?"

"No, I was up. Drinking coffee. Want some?"

"Coffee? No thanks."

"Come in." Lily was glad to. She'd never been inside this cottage before and saw comfortable furniture, beige sofas and chairs, and a businesslike desk with a computer, printer, and lots of paper on it.

"Neat computer," Lily said, running her fingers over the top of the monitor. The papers on the desk were full of scratched-out places and funny-looking equations.

Mrs. Herbert brought her some orange juice. "Here. Try this. I was up late last night getting started on my articles."

Lily pointed at the funny-looking numbers. "What's that stuff?"

"Calculus."

"*Calculus?* You have to do that?" Lily had known there was math in astronomy, but calculus seemed excessive.

"Sure. You like math?"

"Well, I"—Lily squirmed—"changed schools and got pretty lost in multiplication of fractions and percents. But we did some pre-algebra and that was fun."

"Math is fun once you get past the hard part."

Concerned, Lily asked, "What hard part?"

"Fractions."

"Aw, come on."

"I suppose you have to have a knack for it. And an open mind." The woman trailed off to the bedroom. "And good teachers!"

Teachers, Lily thought. Right. And here I am, still not in school, getting behind already.

Mrs. Herbert emerged in her swimming suit, and they walked down to the water. On the way Lily glanced at the woman and grinned to herself. It was nice to have a friend who was an absolute, utter grown-up. It's because of the beach, Lily thought, realizing friendship with a grown woman might not be so easy again. Especially not with Flora Maxwell.

"Hey, look!" Mrs. Herbert called, pointing upward.

A string of pelicans—seven or eight—came flying by, low and slow, their wings barely moving. They turned their heads regally, taking everything in, as if they were kings and queens honoring the landscape with a procession.

Lily watched until they were out of sight. "Aren't they beautiful?"

"They don't look at all like their silly pictures," Mrs. Herbert said. "I like that."

"Me too."

The water was chilly and took Lily's breath away. Mrs. Herbert said, "Brrr. I'm awake now!" and stretched up her arms. "Ahhhhh," she trilled, lifted her feet, sank, and came up laughing.

Lily dunked herself, too. While Mrs. Herbert floated, Lily surfed, then returned and lay on her back, letting the water hold her.

When their swim was done, the two went to shore and dried their faces. Lily's towel was so incredibly grungy she just sort of touched it, figuring the air would dry her better.

"Ah, Mrs. Herbert?"

"Yes?"

"I think we'll be leaving tomorrow. My father's supposed to come."

"Oh? Then you'll be in school? I'd been wondering."

"Yes . . . somewhere."

"You don't know where?"

"No, but"—Lily realized she had a very good guess—"if I know my father, it'll be New York. He'd like that and . . . I don't think his other choices worked out."

"Would that be all right with you?"

"Well . . . sure. I'll just jump in."

"Leap before you look again?"

"Why not?" Lily grinned. "Sometimes it works."

Mrs. Herbert nodded. "There's a poem by Auden that says, 'Look if you like, but you will have to leap.'"

Lily thought about it. "I like that."

"Me too."

They looked at each other. Lily didn't want to have to say good-bye to Mrs. Herbert. "I'll see you."

"Yes." Mrs. Herbert draped a towel over her shoulder. "Guess I better get back to my papers."

"You gonna get them done?"

"Eventually. Though I'd still rather stargaze."

"Right from here? Is that astronomy?"

"Naw, inertia."

Lily watched until Mrs. Herbert was all the way inside, then drifted along the beach toward home, eyes down, searching for shark's teeth. There was a small bed of stones and rubble the tide had turned up, and in it Lily found a small one, just the size of a fingernail.

Nice, she thought, rinsing it off. The tooth was small, flat, perfect. It gave Lily an idea.

She trotted to the house, spilled out her cups of fossils, and chose the smallest ones.

Then she put her paintings flat on the floor, carefully selected black teeth, switching them around until they seemed right. The last painting really only needed one tooth; the others both required three.

Lily hesitated.

Dad would never do this. He's too serious. Well, okay . . .

Mrs. Phipps?

Mrs. Phipps will be mad no matter what.

These are mine. Do I want shark's teeth on them?

Lily grinned. She found the Superglue in the paint box, dribbled some on, then: *zap*, stuck.

She put the first painting against the window. It made her laugh. "I dub thee goofier," she told it, and did the next one. Then the last, adding one small tooth on the dark sand as a kind of signature.

Her father always signed his paintings, OJM. So, these were different.

Through with art, she closed the door to the studio. A car went by on the road and Lily stilled, listening.

Cut it out, she ordered. Mrs. Phipps will come when she comes. Quit worrying.

Late in the afternoon, Lily washed her hair, put on a pink sundress, and made a half-hearted attempt to find her tube of mascara. It was lost. My mother would never not know where her mascara is . . . and Anna Herbert probably doesn't have any.

Lily peered in the mirror at her reflection. The face that peered back had big eyes, even without dark lashes. She decided she looked fine and left, feeling very grown up to be going by herself to a party up the beach.

At the Blakes' a bar was set up on the dining room table. It was stocked with every kind of liquor, three ice buckets, and underneath, two coolers of beer and soda. Graham stood in the living room near a bookcase. When he saw that Lily was alone, he pulled a glass from behind a shelf and toasted her. "Eighteen-year-old whiskey," he said. "Cheers."

Claire and Joey were in the kitchen making sandwiches. "Lily! Thank goodness," Claire greeted her. "Can you help?"

"Sure." They made a production line. Joey cut circles from bread using a cookie cutter. Lily smeared them with cream cheese or salmon paste. Claire decorated the tops with olive or cucumber circles or piles of khaki-green capers from a jar.

Only a counter separated the kitchen from the rest of the main floor, so Lily could see the whole room. When Dr. Blake came in, adjusting his tie, Graham was standing innocently by the sofa.

"All set, kids?" the doctor asked. "How are the sandwiches coming?"

"Good," said Claire.

"Fine." Her father surveyed the bar. "Graham, will you make sure to replace bottles as they get low? And keep the ice buckets full?"

Graham gave him a big, open smile. "I sure will, Dad."

"Thanks. It helps a lot if I have an assistant bartender."

Graham gave the kids in the kitchen a big wink behind his father's back, and Lily whispered to Claire, "Will Graham be all right?"

"He better be. Shh!"

Dr. Blake came into the kitchen, complimented the sandwich crew, and poured peanuts and cashews into bowls. "I think we're set. Right, Graham?"

"Yes sir."

With everything ready, they waited. Dr. Blake paced from the window above the street, to the deck, round and round the room. "I hate the minutes before a party," he complained. "It's like before surgery." He flexed his fingers. "I'd rather . . . be in the middle of it."

Gross, Lily thought, but didn't say so.

The first car arrived, and within ten minutes, thirty people. Cars scrunched outside, voices called, the glass doors of the beach house rolled open and shut, upstairs and down. Guy came in from the ocean side. "Hi," Lily exclaimed, delighted to see him. He had a florist's bouquet that he presented to Claire with a flourish.

"Thank you." Blushing, Claire placed the flowers in a tall vase. "Put some water in, Lily, will you?" She ran to greet a pack of newcomers.

Lily put the flowers near the window, then heard a familiar voice. "Heaven! A divine evening. Enchanting."

Lily froze. Mrs. Phipps! I forgot she'd be here!

The woman swept into the room wearing a slinky strapless dress, her hair wound in a matching turban. "Why, it's our little Maxwell," she cooed at Lily. "How are you, dear?"

"F-fine."

"Come meet my friends." She introduced Lily to five or six people. "Now." The lady licked her lips. "Where is your darling father?"

"Uh." Lily was dumbstruck. She had no story prepared; she was sick to death of lying. "Ah . . ."

Guy rescued her. "He—he's not able to come. You won't believe what happened." He chuckled and winked at Lily. "O.J. went swimming and hurt his foot. Either stepped on a piece of glass or a sharp shell or a crab bit him or . . . Hmm, blood all over the place."

Guy had everyone's attention, the whole room, and Lily thought, He's got too much imagination. Better stop him. "It wasn't that bad."

He glanced at her sheepishly. "No. But we decided he might need stitches. He drove himself to Wilmington. To the doctor."

"Why we have a doctor right here." Mrs. Phipps wiggled her fingers at Dr. Blake. Then she squinted at Lily and waved her glass. "Get us a tray of those nice sandwiches, that's a girl."

Lily was glad to oblige. In the kitchen she found Graham and asked, "Would you take some sandwiches to Mrs. Phipps?"

The boy saluted. His eyes were glittery, his cheeks red. "Sure thing, kiddo." He giggled.

"Graham!" Dr. Blake called. "Ice!"

"Sure thing, Daddo." He got a plastic bowl and went to the refrigerator to scoop ice from a ten-pound bag. Some of it spilled on the floor, and Lily hurried to help him.

"Graham, you better take it easy."

"Yeah." Suddenly he sat right on the spilled ice. Lily finished filling the bowl. She grabbed a plate of sandwiches and delivered them to Mrs. Phipps, explaining that she had to help Dr. Blake as an excuse to escape.

Back in the kitchen, Graham hadn't moved. Lily handed him a damp towel. "Here. Wash your face. Are you okay?"

"Cold," he said, puzzled.

"Well, you're sitting on ice cubes."

"Oh." He moved and she picked most of them up. "Thanks. I . . . think I'll lay off the booze for a while."

He had a lost-little-boy look in his eyes, and she touched his shoulder. "Do that, please?"

"Graham!" his father called.

He swayed to his feet. "Coming."

Lily moved to a chair by the ocean window and watched the party. Claire was happy and sociable, talking to some people near the sofa. Dr. Blake moved smoothly from group to group, a perfect host. He kept Graham close, unconscious of his son's condition. Joey was nowhere in sight. Mrs. Phipps, too, had disappeared.

Must be outside, Lily thought. Guy was standing against a wall deep in conversation with a group of men and women who seemed to hang on his every word.

Then Mrs. Phipps returned, brushing off her feet and putting on her shoes. She saw Lily, smiled hugely, and beckoned. Lily's heart stopped. "Well, young lady," said Mrs. Phipps grandly. "I did it."

"Did it?" Lily quaked, afraid she knew what Mrs. Phipps meant. She didn't . . . find her key?

Mrs. Phipps waved a key in Lily's face. "Yes. Went into your cottage."

Mrs. Phipps didn't look angry. She said, "I told you he was good." Behind her on both sides, her friends all nodded, bobbing their heads at Lily. Mrs. Phipps bent toward her. "Now tell me. What are those murky scenes?"

Lily went to stand by Guy for courage. She suspects, Lily thought, and blurted, "I made them."

"I knew it. Of course. The work of a beginner. Talented, but a student."

Lily's heart resumed beating, fast. She held her breath as Mrs. Phipps went on. "Your father's are different. So much humor, such charm. I love them. I knew he'd hit his stride."

"They're great," said the small round man. "Where is he?"

They like my abstracts, Lily thought, confused. Beside her, Guy took hold of Lily's elbow, though it was unclear which of them needed holding up.

Mrs. Phipps rubbed her hands together. "I wish that great man were here. I'd like to congratulate him, to talk to him." She was bubbling. "They are fascinating. Bold. Amusing. Just what I'd expect of my Mr. Maxwell. Once he got that foolishness out of his system." Her friends nodded and smiled.

Lily said, "Even with the shark's teeth?"

"Of course. What a delightful touch. Shark's teeth aren't everywhere, you know. Makes the paintings from *here*. Obviously for me. I don't suppose he'd put my name on them, would he?"

Lily's ears were ringing; she was dizzy. "No."

"I thought not. Because they're really beyond me, beyond any one person. Just . . . lovely."

Lily fought down a temptation to blurt out everything, to say, But I made them. They're mine! The whole idea had been for Mrs. Phipps not to know O.J. was gone. It had worked. Don't ruin it, she told herself. "Th-thank you, Mrs. Phipps. He'll be pleased," she managed to say, and fled.

She ran outside to the deck, down the stairs, across the lower deck to the beach stairs. She brushed past someone—Joey—and went on, down across the sand to the water.

"They're mine!" she shouted at the waves, then kicked off her sandals and waded in. The water was warm around her feet, the ocean dark except at the last minute, when a wave lifted and came rushing close.

I never expected her to like them. She thinks they're O.J.'s. Does that mean she wants them? Can I let her?

What am I going to do?

Lily's feet were sinking; the water kept coming. She stepped backward a few steps to get on firmer ground.

She hadn't started painting in order for this to happen.

"If I were an artist," she whispered to the sea, uncertain of everything, "I wouldn't do things this way. . . ."

After awhile a small voice behind her said, "Lily?" It was Joey. "Are you all right? Why are you standing there?"

"Oh, Joey," she said, glad to see him. "Did you ever know how—when things work out, they get all mixed up?"

In the darkness she could see him shake his head. "Maybe I'm too little."

"Lucky you." She found her sandals. "Let's go back and sit on the steps."

Joey held her hand all the way across the sand. They started up the stairs and Lily saw Guy, standing at the top.

"Lily! I was looking for you."

"I'm right here."

"You ran away so fast. I was so shocked. What a victory." He bent down and whispered, "What did you do to those paintings?"

"They're like what you saw. I just . . . stuck on some shark's teeth."

He must have seen her face for he said, "Are you all right?"

"Sure. I'm in shock."

"Okay. See you later." He disappeared.

Lily and Joey sat a few steps from the top, where no one could see them. Lily leaned back on her elbows and Joey patted her knee. "You looked awfully sad out there."

"I'm all right." Lily changed the subject. "What

about you? Will you be okay at that school tomorrow?"

"I think so. Claire says new things are more bad beforehand."

"She's right. And you'll have her and Graham both there with you."

"They forget me."

Lily could imagine how true that was. "I bet."

"Daddy said I could always call him. Or Momma."

"And you'll meet people you like."

"You think so?"

"Guaranteed."

They were pushed apart by Graham, who slipped between them and ran down the steps to the beach. At the bottom they could hear him throwing up.

"Graham's dumb," said Joey.

"No kidding."

"Graham?" Dr. Blake called from the upper sliding glass door. "You out here?"

"Uh-oh. I better go." Joey stood. "Take his place."

"Ata boy," said Lily. She stayed where she was, watching the night, and soon Graham came up and collapsed beside her.

"Boy, I feel awful." In the dim light he was pale green.

"I can tell."

"Don't know what gets into me. I'll probably be an alcoholic by the time I'm fourteen."

"That would be terrible."

156

"It's fun for the first half hour, then yecch." He turned to glance at the house. "Dad find out?"

"Not yet. Joey went in to cover for you."

"Ahh." He leaned his head against the rail. "Feel dizzy."

"Graham, do me a favor?"

"What?"

"Stop for tonight. Don't have any more."

He put his head in his hands. "Okay. Why not." A minute later, in a soft voice, he added, "At Christmas we saw him for two days. I barfed all over his feet. He . . . says he trusts me now."

Then why don't you act trustworthy? . . . Because he doesn't really see you? Doesn't know the difference? She didn't understand the Blakes and could only say, "On his feet? Yuk."

"It was bad." He gave a big sigh, then jabbed Lily in the ribs. "Want to go skinny-dipping?"

"No." They sat quietly. The sky was so high there were a million stars, and Lily found herself wishing this moment could last forever. Even with Graham.

Then she noticed that standing alone above her was Mrs. Phipps.

"Stay here, Graham. I'll be right back," Lily whispered. She went up and joined the woman. "Hello, Mrs. Phipps."

"Hello . . . little Maxwell."

"Enjoying the party?"

"Of course." She kept on looking outward, though

it was too dark to see. "Owen knows how to do things right."

"Mmm." Lily glanced down at Graham and thought, Some things. "Ah, Mrs. Phipps?"

"Hmm?" the lady said, sounding mellow.

"I just want to say thank you. For having us here this summer. I loved it."

"Well!" Mrs. Phipps seemed surprised, as if usually no one thanked her for things. "You're welcome. My pleasure."

12 · Saturday

～～～～～～～～～～～～～～～

Lily went back to the stairs. There was Graham, asleep. He stirred and groaned when she approached. "Ohhhhh," he said, sitting up. "I feel awful. Better go to bed."

"G'night, Graham," Lily said. He seemed very pitiful.

He struggled to stand, swayed, and went upward.

Lily stayed on the steps. Behind her the sounds of the party rose and fell, disappeared into the wind and surf, then returned in a burst of laughter.

After awhile Guy came. "I thought I'd find you here."

Lily stirred. "Yes. I . . . guess I got hypnotized." She reached out to the water, up to the sky. "Like Mrs. Herbert. There's so many stars."

Guy looked, too. "Sky's never been so clear."

"What happened in there?" Lily glanced back at the house. "Did Mrs. Phipps leave? Did you see Graham?"

"Mrs. Phipps and Howard Best—"

"The small round man?"

"Yes. They got into a terrible fight about airline regulation. You'd think they were in charge. Graham came in and went to sleep in a chair."

"He was drinking."

"I thought so. Owen doesn't realize." Guy took a step downward. "I'm ready to go. You too?"

"Yes." Lily ran up to say good-night, then walked with Guy the short distance between houses. They passed his cottage and continued on to Lily's stairs.

"Dad said he'd call after the show," Lily said.

"I'll blink the lights. Will you see?"

"I'll wait." Lily reached out and touched Guy's hand. "Thank you, Guy. You're such a good friend." He bowed, and Lily remembered how he'd bowed to Claire when he presented the flowers. "You're very fancy tonight."

"It's parties," he explained. "They affect me that way. Particularly if I wasn't really keen on going."

He went home. In the cottage Lily discovered that Mrs. Phipps and her group had left tracks: a sandwich plate on the floor, a cocktail glass on a table, sand all over.

As Lily continued into the studio, she imagined the intruders walking around, looking at everything. They'd strewn a kind of exhibition along the wall: all of Lily's paintings, acrylics and oils both; O.J.'s dumb-and-ugly; and, finally, from the closet, the last of O.J.'s real paintings—the one that had been too wet to move.

Lily put it back in the closet, propped her two oils against the far wall, and thought, People shouldn't be allowed to come into houses this way, even if they do own them.

She turned off the lights, went to the deck where she sat on a chair with her feet on the rail, and waited until Guy's phone rang and the lights began to blink. Then she hurried across the sand and wheezed, "Dad?"

"Hi, honey. How are you?"

"Fine. How are you? How'd it go?"

"Lily, it was "—he paused—"amazing. I wish you'd been there. There were critics from two big magazines and the *Times*. Somebody heard one of them say, 'This is good work.' "

"No." Lily could imagine the people, the talk. She was happy for him. "Really?"

"Yes. Five canvases sold within two hours. And I've got a commission to do a mural on the mezzanine of the Plaza. I still don't believe it."

"That's wonderful."

"So get us packed up, will you? I'm leaving in a few minutes. We've got to get right back. We're moving to New York."

"Packed? So soon? New York?"

"We'll sublet Denny's friend's loft and . . . I've been finding out about schools."

Lily had predicted they'd move to New York, but

now the reality began to sink in. She'd been to Denny's before but hadn't paid a lot of attention. "Where is it? What kind of neighborhood?"

"Downtown, in Soho. Fascinating."

Lily gulped. "Sounds terrific."

"It will be. Oh, Lily, we'll be settled again at last."

"Okay, Dad. See you tomorrow. Be careful."

When she hung up, she repeated the conversation to Guy, and he said, "I'm glad you'll be in New York. When I come up to see my publisher, I'll visit you."

He yawned, and Lily said, "Go to sleep," and went home.

In her own cottage, she wasn't at all tired. She turned on every light, walked from room to room, and thought, What do I have to do? What do I . . . want to do?

She had one last bit of precious time. Things needed to be concluded or they'd slip away.

Mother.

She got the packet of letters, a clean sheet of paper and an envelope, sat at the dining room table, and wrote a letter.

Dear Mother,

We are still at the beach, but we'll be moving to New York soon. How about a one-week visit sometime? That's what people here seem to do, and it works. They get to know each other. At school this year I'm going to pay a lot more attention in math. Because I'm thinking of becoming an astronomer. Sorry this is so short. It's the middle of the night.

> Love,
> Lily

She sealed the letter, addressed it, and went to the studio.

I still don't feel right about Mrs. Phipps, Lily said to herself as she looked at her abstracts. She picked up the first—her favorite—and carried it and the letter across the sand to Guy's.

The lights were out. She knocked anyway, and he came to the door in his pajamas.

"Hi," Lily said. "Were you asleep?"

"Not quite," he answered, rubbing his eyes.

"Oh. Good. Can I come in?" She knew she was bothering him, but right now she couldn't help it.

"Sure, what's up?" He opened the door wider. He was wearing blue-and-white-striped seersucker pajamas and said, "Wait a minute," and came back with a bathrobe on, too.

"I just wanted to ask if you would mail this letter for me." She handed over the envelope. "It needs foreign postage—" Guy read the name and nodded. "And"—she balanced her painting on a chair—"I want to give you this."

"For me? But—" He stepped back, suddenly wide awake, his head tilted to one side. "I do like it."

"The shark's teeth don't ruin it?"

"No. I'd thought they might. Instead, they sort of make it . . ." He didn't have the word.

"Goofy?"

"In a nice way."

"That's what I think, too."

"Of course, the teeth do"— he was very serious now—"take the eye away from the form, and the form was what was really special. So they do . . . dilute it."

Lily looked again. "That's why Dad wouldn't use them."

"Probably. But I like it anyway. There's such humor, exuberance."

Lily bent her head, embarrassed. Then she straightened. "That's why I want you to have it."

"But what about Mrs. Phipps?"

"She'll have to be mad. I—" Lily nodded at her painting, touched a corner of the canvas. "This picture is like a promise." She saw from Guy's face that he understood. "It isn't a promise if Mrs. Phipps has it. If she thinks it's O.J.'s."

"I'm honored," said Guy, embarrassing her all over again. "I'll keep your promise."

"Not that I'm necessarily going to be an artist, you know."

"I know. It's much too soon to tell."

"Right."

Lily went home, turned off the lights, and went to sleep.

* * *

She woke later than usual. The morning was bright and crisp; no one was out. Lily made some tea and threw all her clothes, then her father's, into two well-worn suitcases. She put them by the door, next to pillowcases full of dirty clothes. Then rummaged in the storeroom under the house for cardboard cartons and started on the kitchen.

New York, she thought, piling corn flakes and tomato sauce into a box. Seems awfully sudden. Am I ready? What if I don't like it? When I'm grown up and can live anywhere, where would I pick? San Francisco? Here? She turned slowly. Who knows?

A knock at the door interrupted her. It was Claire. "We're going. Come say good-bye?"

They walked on the highway instead of the beach. Dr. Blake's car was crammed full. He shook Lily's hand. Graham seemed groggy. His smile wobbled. "See you later, shark meat."

"Graham." She shoved his shoulder. "Grow up."

"Guess what?" said Claire, giving Lily the third in a series of dramatic farewell hugs. "Daddy's going to buy me some Flora Maxwell jewelry. Aren't you?"

"When you're sixteen, angel," he promised, then turned to Lily hopefully. "Does it ever go on sale?"

"You mean marked down? I don't think so." Lily smiled, thinking, He buys her off. She gets him to. That's not what I'd want.

Joey gave her a perfect sand dollar he'd been saving,

and Lily said, "Joey, don't change. You're perfect."

The Blakes climbed into the car; the engine roared. Lily called, "Good luck with the tryout, Claire! Good-bye Graham, Joey, good luck!"

Claire stuck her head out the window as they pulled away. "Write me!"

"I will!" Lily patted the pocket where she'd put the address. "Good-bye everybody!"

She stayed in the street and waved until they were out of sight, then turned toward home.

A car swooshed by her fast, then braked and turned into Lily's driveway. It was Mrs. Phipps's Cadillac. Oh no!

Lily started running and noticed something else: Guy's car tucked under his house. And Dad!

She caught Mrs. Phipps rounding the top stair at the front of the house. O.J. was standing on the deck, shielding his eyes as if looking for someone down on the beach.

"Mr. Maxwell!"

"Lily! Here you are!"

"Daddy!"

Lily dashed around Mrs. Phipps, tackled her father's middle, and hugged him tight. "Oh Dad, you're here! Be careful," she whispered. "She doesn't suspect."

O.J. was grinning and didn't stop. He kept holding on to Lily, dragging her along as he crossed to Mrs. Phipps, reaching out to shake her hand. "Mrs. Phipps.

Nice to see you. Good morning. Care to come in?"
Still he was smiling.

"Why, yes." She smiled, too. O.J.'s enthusiasm
was infectious.

"We'll be leaving today, so we'll want to"—he
touched his pocket—"settle up."

"Yes." Mrs. Phipps lifted her purse. "Very well."

Trying to be unobtrusive, Lily retrieved the key,
unlocked the door, and let Mrs. Phipps go first.

The three of them were moving toward the studio.
Lily thought, I don't know what's going to happen. I
don't like this. . . . She hadn't had time to warn her
father of anything. She hadn't had time to make up her
mind what she was going to do.

Mrs. Phipps stepped into the studio, turned, and
said to O.J., "Mr. Maxwell, these paintings are wonderful."

"W-what?" he said.

Lily pinched his arm. "Be cool."

"What? Let me see." He squeezed past the woman.
The oils were over in a corner; the two remaining
goofys and old dumb-and-ugly stood proudly under
the ocean window. O.J. went close and peered down at
them. He seemed speechless.

Lily didn't know what to say, either.

Mrs. Phipps went to the closet and pulled out
O.J.'s real sea painting. "I might reconsider and take
this one, too."

Lily thought, I bet her friends liked it.

"You—ah—" O.J. was finally—maybe—getting himself together. "I brought . . . I mean—" He looked at Lily and appeared totally befuddled. "Some paintings were delivered today from New York. They're on the deck. Wait." He ran out and returned with two of his canvases from the colony. They depicted fragile-looking red brick chimneys against a web of brown trees and the winter sky.

"Ah, yes. I remember those from when I hired you." Mrs. Phipps stroked her chin, studying them like a critic. "They might make a nice contrast to the sea." She took out her checkbook. "I think we can do business." Then she paused, counting with her eyes. "But there was another of those." She pointed at the abstracts. Lily noticed that every time O.J. looked at them he squinted with puzzlement. "Where's the other one?"

O.J.'s mouth opened but nothing came out.

Lily said, "It was unfinished, remember?"

"But it isn't now. And I like it."

Lily plunged on. "Well, I gave it to Guy Franklin."

"You?"

"Yes." Lily took a deep breath. She was finally sure of what she wanted to do. "Mrs. Phipps, you can take the other two if you want them. But you don't have to pay. Because they're mine."

"Yours? Are you an artist?"

168

Maybe, Lily told herself. Right now, anyway. She took a small step forward. "Yes."

"Well!" Mrs. Phipps blinked and held tight to her checkbook.

O.J. remained speechless.

Mrs. Phipps seemed to think of something and glared at O.J., wrinkling her nose in distaste. "If she made these paintings," she said fiercely, "then what have you been doing all week? Sitting around? Walking on the beach? Letting this young lady do all the work? Shame on you!"

O.J. spread his hands and said, "Uhhhh—"

"All right, then!" Mrs. Phipps was suddenly all business again. "My friends were marvelously impressed. I've had some unexpected expenses with my building. It's just as well that you don't have so many pictures for me. I'll take these four"—dumb-and-ugly, the real sea painting, the two chimney-sky's—"and pay for them. And take those two"—she pointed at Lily's—"for my trouble. You have been trouble, you know."

O.J. nodded.

Lily said, "What will you do with them? Mine?"

"Hang them. On"—the woman's lips twitched into a smile—"on . . . somewhat less important walls."

Lily found she couldn't help smiling back.

"Good," said Mrs. Phipps. She wrote the check, marking it *Account Paid in Full.* "Wonderful. Now, if you'll help me load these. That's a dear man. By the way, how's your foot?"

"Foot." O.J. clearly had no idea what she meant. (Lily thought, He's supposed to have had stitches. There he is walking fine . . . in his sneakers!) He studied his feet, then shrugged at his patron. "My feet are great. Thank you."

Mrs. Phipps frowned. "My, you artists are tough," she said. "Leave the key on the table when you go. It's been a pleasure doing business with you." The paintings loaded, she called, "Toodle-oo!" and was gone.

Back inside, O.J. grabbed Lily in a bear hug, lifted her, and whirled through the cottage. "How did you do that? You're wonderful!"

He put her down in the studio and crouched before the oils. "You made these? They're not bad, not really. I never knew you were interested in painting."

"I didn't, either." Lily didn't know what else to say.

"And those others—"

"She thought they were yours."

"With shark's teeth?"

"I knew you would never do that. That's why I put them on. But then . . . I had to tell her."

"Amazing." He reached out his arms as if to enfold her again. "Well, now. Tell me everything."

He was expectant. His hair was messy and there were circles under his eyes. He drove all night, Lily realized. Hasn't even had a nap. "Aren't you sleepy?"

"It'll hit me after we get going. When it does, we'll stop in a motel. Agree?"

"Okay." Lily went into the living room and he followed. Her father seemed so big, he overfilled the cottage. Everywhere she looked O.J. was there. She realized she wasn't used to him. "I . . . in a minute."

"Okay." He rubbed his hair, seeming confused. "Guy's making us some breakfast. Um, have you packed?"

"No. Yes." Lily glared at her father. He was becoming a little less like a stranger. More irritating. "Whaddaya think!" she exploded. "I can't do everything, you know."

"B-b—" he began.

Lily bit her lips to keep from laughing and forced herself not to run to him with a hug.

"You get started, Dad. I'm going outside."

From the deck she saw new people on the beach—weekenders.

I'll explain things as we drive, Lily decided. We can drive for miles—hours—talking. Lily had a lot to tell. She knew the hard part would be Flora. What could she say? I wrote to her. Lily was afraid her father wouldn't understand. He had his own silences, hurts with Flora Maxwell.

I have to keep me separate.

The sea swished and glittered. Lily stood very still, memorizing it. She knew that wherever she went she would carry this place, these people, with her. They were part of her now.

Mrs. Herbert was in the water.

Lily turned to the cottage and called, "Hey Dad. Come on. Let's go for one last swim. Are you ready?"